S0-AGM-251

Daily Meditations (with Scripture) for Busy Parents

Daily Meditations (with Scripture) for Busy Parents

Tom McGrath

ACTA

ASSISTING CHRISTIANS TO ACT

PUBLICATIONS

Daily Meditations (with Scripture) for Busy Parents
by Tom McGrath

Edited by Gregory F. Augustine Pierce
Proofread by Andrew Yankech
Artwork by Isz
Cover design by Tom A. Wright
Typesetting by Desktop Edit Shop, Inc.

Scripture quotations are from the *New Revised Standard Version of the Bible,* copyright © 1989 by the Division of Christian Education of the National Council of the Churches of Christ in the U.S.A. Used with permission. All rights reserved.

Copyright © 2002 by Tom McGrath

Published by: ACTA Publications
                Assisting Christians To Act
                4848 N. Clark Street
                Chicago, IL 60640-4711
                773-271-1030
                actapublications@aol.com

All rights reserved. No part of this publication may be reproduced or transmitted in any form or by any means, electronic or mechanical, including photocopying and recording, or by any information storage and retrieval system, without permission from the publisher.

Library of Congress Catalog Number: 2002092796

ISBN: 0-87946-236-1

Printed in the United States of America
Year: 08 07 06 05 04 03 02
Printing: 10 9 8 7 6 5 4 3 2 1

Contents

January / 11

February / 31

March / 49

April / 69

May / 89

June / 111

July / 131

August / 153

September / 173

October / 193

November / 213

December / 235

Dedication

In gratitude for Kathleen and her golden heart.

Introduction

These snippets of meditation come from various ages and stages in my life as a parent. Some I experienced myself; others were shared with me by other parents. My hope is that these daily reflections will open your eyes and your heart to the wonder of childrearing as a rich spiritual practice and your very own spiritual path.

In the gospels, Jesus told the story of the end of the world, when we will be asked: "When did we see you hungry and feed you? When did we see you thirsty and give you to drink? When were you naked and we clothed you?" Parents have the opportunity to practice these works of mercy every day. We can either perform them blindly and unreflectively or we can awaken to the spiritual opportunities in our midst.

This book is intended to give you eyes to see the grand adventure you are having with your children. May you open your heart to the abundant life that awaits you and those you love so dearly and so well.

January 1   All things new

J esus, you said, "Behold, I make all things new." I notice you didn't say, "I make all new things." You seem content to bring about the reign of God using the raw materials at your disposal—including us parents.

I know how everything about raising kids can change in the blink of an eye, how the world can be transformed from a valley of shadows to a joyous, golden banquet. When I tap into your love, everything in my family life is renewed, even though nothing else has changed.

In this New Year, Lord, help me stay connected to you. Help me to be a channel of your love and peace to my children, those special people I love so much.

> *From this time forward I make you hear new*
> *things, hidden things that you have not known.*
> **Isaiah 48:6**

January 2   Keep or toss?

T he beginning of a new year is a great time to evaluate what to keep and what to leave behind.

Things to leave behind this year:

- remorse for things we've already regretted and repented;
- resentment for slights more than two weeks old;
- gossip that needn't be spread any further;
- prejudices that shrink and limit our world;
- internal messages that tell us "you can't do it;"
- habits of unrealistic fear;
- reliance on things rather than people to make life worthwhile.

Things to keep this year:

- memories of times we really connected with our children;
- commitment to our principles;
- our sense of humor;
- our sense of gratitude;
- faith that God cares for parents even in the hardest times;
- hope that light will always overcome darkness;
- love that helps us see the face of God in our children;
- the conviction that, despite possible indications to the contrary, all is well.

> *He rained down on them manna to eat, and*
> *gave them the grain of heaven.*
>
> **Psalm 78:24**

January 3 — Snow angels

S now falls gently all day, thick flakes tumbling around us. My children and I don our winter gear and head out to play, building snowmen and a snow slide and piling up a stock of snowballs. The day unfolds softly with the fragility of a snowflake—unique, intricate and passing.

As night falls, the snow continues to drift down. I peek in on my two snow angels who lay in bed now, pink cheeks on warm pillows. I'm keenly aware that all day long, grace tumbled down amid the snowflakes.

How can I praise you enough, God, for allowing me to be a parent?

> *Praise him all his angels; praise him all his host!*
>
> **Psalm 148:2**

January 4   Hot potato

I wake up feeling anxious. Being uncomfortable, I pass my anxiety on to my kids by harping on some minor infraction. They begin to spat and quibble among themselves. Their mother picks up on it and enters the fray.

Sometimes our life together is like a game of hot potato, though instead of a potato we pass around our anxiety, anger or fear.

God, help me to deal with my emotions in a healthier way and not use my kids as a dumping ground. Help me to withhold the drama and the trauma and simply give them my non-anxious presence.

If there's a hot potato in our family, remind us to drop it in your lap and ask your help to live sanely. I think we're all a little tired of getting burned.

> *Here am I and the children whom God has given me.*
>
> **Hebrews 2:13**

January 5   Afraid of the dark

My kids are afraid to go down in the basement on their own. I understand. I was afraid of the dark myself at their age. And so I accompany them when they want to retrieve a toy or game from the basement. Having had my own dark times, I've come to realize that there can be deep and abiding blessings when we confront and overcome our shadows.

I know every inch of this house. I know what's causing the strange noises, those eerie sounds in the night. What I'm really afraid of is what awaits my children when they go out into the world without me. That's the darkness that scares me now.

> *We wait for light, and lo! there is darkness.*
>
> **Isaiah 59:9**

January 6 — Wisdom

Today's the feast of the three wise men. We call it Little Christmas, the feast of the Epiphany.

The magi must have been surprised when they arrived at the end of their quest. Instead of a king, they found two parents and their vulnerable baby, huddling in a stable. I'm sure many people walked right by this poor family, never noticing their plight.

What we parents seek is what we will find. If we're looking for riches and comfort and ease, we might not see the greatest gift of all—the infant in a manger who came to be bread for the world, nourishment for all, who is reflected in our own children.

God give us the eyes to see.

> *Wise men from the East came to Jerusalem asking, "Where is the child who has been born king of the Jews?"*

Matthew 2:2

January 7 — A little catch-up

I heard about a tribe of nomads. After covering a good bit of ground, their custom was to stop and sit quietly. They were letting their souls get a chance to catch up with them.

From time to time we each need that kind of "catch-up" time for our soul.

Today, for instance. It was a great holiday season for my family and me, but it took its toll emotionally and spiritually. It's not that what happened was bad, but I feel as though I've gotten ahead of my soul and it needs a chance to catch up. Sometime today I will take a bit of time to sit in silence and simply wait. That kind of quiet time can be hard to find, but it doesn't take long for "soul catch-up" to occur.

*Happy is the one who listens to me, watching
daily at my gates, waiting beside my doors.*

Proverbs 8:34

January 8   The next right thing

God, I don't want to be the adult anymore. I want somebody else to worry about the bills on the kitchen table, the strange noise emanating from under the hood of my car, and the message from the teacher saying, "Please return this call; it's important."

Some days the biggest act of faith I can muster as a parent is to simply do what's in front of me with some sense of patience and hope, to not snap at the store clerks or phone receptionists or the people closest to me, my family. Today, the best I can muster is to do the next right thing. The rest is up to you, God.

**Be still before the Lord and wait patiently for
him.**

Psalm 37:7

January 9   Bridge over troubled waters

Walking home from work, I see a woman and her child. They're sitting together on the bridge over the Chicago River, exposed to the biting wind and glares of passersby. I fumble in my pocket and find a few coins and a wrinkled dollar bill.

I think of how hard it is to hold together my own home and family, and I have a willing and able partner in that task. I remember what it took, years ago, to pull together the security deposit on our first apartment. I remember all the demoralizing job interviews and the pain it took to establish credit and a community of friends and support as we started our life together.

Later at home, sitting on the couch with my kids, I hug them close to me as I hear the wind howl outside. I wonder where that mother and young child have landed for the night.

> *On entering the house they saw the child with*
> *Mary his mother. And they knelt down and paid*
> *him homage.*

Matthew 2:11

January 10   Lamentations

I've blown it, Lord. I let resentments build and then my temper flared. I can think of a million reasons for my outburst, but no real justifications. I'm keenly aware of my failings as a husband and a dad.

I want to throw in the towel, but that would be taking the easy way out.

Help me to practice the discipline of picking up and starting over again. I'll admit my mistake, ask forgiveness, and do what is needed to avoid this happening again. The good news is, I know my family is always ready to reconcile. The only question is, will I be mature enough to accept their forgiveness?

> *Have mercy on us, O Lord, have mercy on us.*

Psalm 123:3

January 11   Pretty

My daughters and their girl friends are playing dress-up in the attic, donning clothes and jewelry that have spent years in storage. "Aren't I pretty?" asks a tiny, sweet voice. They all want to be grown up.

Of course they are pretty in their oversized high heels and gaudy necklaces and scarves and bracelets. But they're more than pretty. Far more. I think of the line from Roberta Bondi, "'Pretty' has no more to do with 'beautiful' than 'nice' has to do with 'good.'"

I understand the girls' longing to be pretty, because the world pays attention to those who are. But I ache for them to know a truth that's far more important: how beautiful they are—and always will be—on the inside.

God, give my children the eyes to see their inner beauty in years to come.

> *One thing I asked of the Lord, that will I seek*
> *after: to live in the house of the Lord all the days*
> *of my life, to behold the beauty of the Lord, and*
> *to inquire in his temple.*

Psalm 27:4

January 12   The business trip

Was it just yesterday that I was mumbling to myself that I can never get a minute's peace and quiet at home? Why can't everyone just let me read my newspaper in peace?

It's been a long day of travel and meetings and phone calls and faxes. I get to my hotel room and the door bangs shut behind me. Suddenly, I can physically feel the absence of noise. I sit on the edge of the bed, aware of just how much I ache for my family.

> *O Lord, all my longing is known to you; my*
> *sighing is not hidden from you.*

Psalm 38:9

January 13   Out for drinks

He senses the excitement in the group getting ready to leave work together. They're going out for drinks and camaraderie. "Wanna come?" they ask.

"No," he says. "Not tonight." Tuition for the kids was due last week and the car's exhaust is sounding funny. Cash flow is tight, but that's not his main reason for heading home. He doesn't try to explain to his colleagues that he and his wife had made a pact when their first child arrived that they would both try to be home every night for dinner.

They consider this practice to be their most promising investment as a couple...and as a couple of parents.

> ***For where your treasure is, there your heart will be also.***
>
> **Matthew 6:21**

January 14   Disillusionment

I heard a spiritual guru describe how disciples must go through a process of breaking down their illusions in order to make spiritual progress. I laughed and thought of my friend Sharon, who once told me about a less-than-golden moment with her sons.

She wrote, "We live near some woods, and a skunk somehow got trapped in a window well, right near the furnace's air intake. The furnace went on and the smell went through the whole house. At that point one of my sons called out from his bedroom, 'Mom, are you making something new for dinner again?'"

Being a parent means you'll never have to wait long for your illusions to be shattered.

When pride comes, then comes disgrace; but
wisdom is with the humble.

Proverbs 11:2

January 15   Friends of the family

I learned early in parenthood that I had two types of friends who came over to my house. There were the ones who enjoyed my kids and included them in the conversation and fun, and the ones who all but ignored them. I observed how my children responded to this latter type—either withdrawing coldly or acting up and making the visit miserable.

But with the others, I noticed how my kids blossomed under the wing of these "friends of the family." In fact, I discovered new things about my children by watching them come to life under a new adult's attention.

When an evening with friends was done, I would always whisper a silent prayer. With the ones who had no patience for my children I usually thanked God that the evening was over. With those who loved the kids, I thanked God for the treasures everyone discovered and shared right under my roof.

Let the little children come to me, and do not
stop them; for it is to such as these that the king-
dom of heaven belongs.

Matthew 19:14

January 16   The tiny voice

One time, my child, you were so sad. You sat on your mother's lap and cried. When the tears subsided but the pain was still there, your mother taught you how to look inside your heart to find out what was hurting and how to help yourself. She taught you to listen to the "tiny voice inside."

When you went off to college, we were glad you packed pictures of your family and had a cell phone to call us. But most of all we were comforted to know that wherever you go you carry that tiny voice inside of you...and know how to listen to it.

> *But the Lord was not in the earthquake. And after the earthquake, a fire. But the Lord was not in the fire. And after the fire, a sound of sheer silence. When Elijah heard this, he wrapped his face in his mantel.*
>
> **1 Kings 19:11-13**

January 17 Time away

It's been a while since I spent time with you, Lord. I see the effects in my life, and they're not good: lack of patience, lack of perspective, ego and fear running wild. How quickly I can lose my way.

A friend tells me he believes his internal compass is about ten percent off. The longer he goes without reorienting himself in prayer, the farther he drifts from your ways.

I'm astounded at how quickly I lose my way as a parent. And I'm humbled at how quickly you welcome me back.

> *Guide our feet into the way of peace.*
>
> **Luke 1:79**

January 18   Messages

When my children started listening to pop music on the radio I strained to understand the lyrics. What I heard appalled me.

So when I listened in as they played in their bedroom one Sunday afternoon, I was gratified to hear them singing, "This is the day the Lord has made, let us rejoice and be glad." We'd sung it at church that morning, and the music (and, I hope, the message) had stuck.

One for our side!

> *Write them on the tablet of your heart.*
>
> **Proverbs 3:3**

January 19   Blazing new trails

My oldest daughter just returned from her first day of work at her chosen career. She's graduated from college and is out in the work world. My baby is now a woman, teaching in a public high school on Chicago's West Side. She loves it.

I can see the energy and excitement in her face as she comes up the walkway to our house, and for some reason I remember her returning from her first day of kindergarten. That night at dinner she talked excitedly about "Jason and Miss Wentink and Jennifer and...." Tonight she's talking excitedly of "Jorge and Lydia and Mr. Guerra the principal and...."

I assume I still have much good work to do in my life, and I am deeply grateful for that. And yet I also know that I am in the home stretch while my child is just beginning. It's a bittersweet feeling. Yet seeing her excitement tonight, I am filled with joy and an abiding gladness that—long after I am gone—she may well be standing amid young hearts and "raising them to the light."

He must increase and I must decrease.

John 3:30

January 20   Good day

I forgot to set the alarm and so my wife, Kathleen, and I woke up a half hour late today. There was pandemonium as four of us scrambled to make up for lost time—and take our turns in the one bathroom.

I can't find the report I worked on last night, and the kids can't find their shoes. Someone knocks over a glass of orange juice and it drips down behind the table and along the kitchen wall. As I clean it up I realize I'm missing yet another train and that I've also knelt in orange juice. We all snipe at one another and get in each other's way.

My wife announces, "Okay, everybody, take a deep breath. Let's all slow down." We each stop and stand a moment right where we are. We ask God for help to turn things around. Kathleen reminds us, "It's never too late to have a good day."

She's right. It just takes me a while to be willing to have one.

He drew me up from the desolate pit, from the
miry bog, and set my feet upon a rock and made
my steps secure.

Psalm 40:2

January 21   Let freedom ring

A merica's greatest gift and greatest challenge is the diversity of its people. Our future, and even more so our children's future, depends on whether the nationalities and the races can live productively in peace. And we will live in peace only to the extent that justice exists in the land. It's tempting to think that if we, personally, do not discriminate or commit acts of prejudice, then we've done all that's necessary. Yet our society is a system, and if built into the system is a basic unfairness for some, justice and peace will not come. Systems are never easy to change.

Martin Luther King, a brave man, a man inspired by a deep faith, pointed the way for us all. Wouldn't it be good if our children inherited a world where problems of racial discord were well on their way to being resolved? Do one thing today to promote racial healing.

> *Now the Lord is the Spirit, and where the Spirit*
> *of the Lord is, there is freedom.*
>
> **2 Corinthians 3:17**

January 22   Zen Master

I grew up afraid of animals, so I never thought I'd see the day I'd share my home with a cat. But one day my wife and I relent, letting our kids bring home a kitten.

Missy the cat earns her keep, however, and has become my Zen master. Her main jobs are two. In the evening when I get into bed, she sits next to me and lets me pet her until she's had enough (and not a minute less). The rest of the day, it seems, she spends seeking out the coziest, most comfortable place in our home and taking long naps.

My fear of animals has eased. I do my share of providing Missy her food, water and a clean litter box. Over time I have grown to love her.

Having an animal in our lives has made me more human, and thus a better parent.

Show me your ways, so that I may know you
and find favor in your sight.

Exodus 33:13

January 23   The waiting game

I'm sorely tempted to go on strike. I don't want to be responsible today. I have all sorts of deadlines, commitments and expectations of others. I want to lie on the couch and watch stupid TV shows all day. Forget my work. Forget my responsibilities to and for the kids.

I'm sorely tempted, but I know that this feeling shall pass. This moment of depression and despair will ease if I will let it. It's hard to wait for good things, Lord. Sometimes it's even harder to wait for bad feelings to just go away.

I waited patiently for the Lord; he inclined to
me and heard my cry.

Psalm 40:1

January 24   Just-in-time delivery

As the day goes on, the kids start wearing on my nerves. It's been cold and bleak, and cabin fever is setting in. We're getting antsy. In the kitchen, one of the girls spills her milk, the glass shattering across the floor.

On my knees, sopping up milk and picking up slivers of glass, I happen to look up at the clock. Ah, three hours more and we'll be dropping them off at Grandma's, where they'll be treated like princesses. My wife and I will go off to a quiet meal with no spills, no arguments, and the chance to speak to one another in complete, uninterrupted, adult sentences.

We'll awake tomorrow morning, missing our children again and eager to retrieve them.

Thank you, God, for extended family.

> **Then we your people, the flock of your pasture,**
> **will give thanks to you forever; from generation**
> **to generation we will recount your praise.**
>
> **Psalm 79:13**

January 25   Passages

L ast week, my mother-in-law came to the reluctant conclusion that it is time for her to move into an assisted living senior residence. It wasn't an easy decision, and she's handling it with her usual grace.

As we made the tour of her new place, I think about how swiftly time passes and how the goodness of the moment can be elusive if we're caught up wishing things were different than they are. My mother-in-law is a tremendous model of faith in the present moment. Though she worries about details of the day, on the larger issue of life's purpose she is teaching us a thing or two about acceptance and trust.

I know that there must be enough grace in this moment for us all, but it is the nature of passages that you often don't recognize where the grace is until you come through the other end of it. And so we all follow her lead and go forward with faith and trust, relying on the love we all have for one another.

> **I am reminded of your sincere faith, a faith that**
> **lived first in your grandmother.**
>
> **2 Timothy 1:5**

January 26   End of the rope

I'll give you something to cry about," the father screamed at his
son, swatting wildly at the bawling toddler in the grocery
store. They'd both obviously reached the end of their ropes.

Passersby turned their heads away, pretending to be absorbed in
the price of breakfast cereal. The dad sat down on the floor in the
middle of the cookie aisle and hung his head. The boy, mystified by
such behavior, quieted down. The dad finally stood, gently pulled
his son out of the seat in the grocery cart, and held him close. At
the checkout counter, the dad put his groceries on the counter with
one hand. His other arm was wrapped around his boy, clasping
him heart-to-heart.

> ***And God will wipe away every tear from their
> eyes.***
>
> **Revelation 7:17**

January 27   Something big

Somehow a dad knows it's time. He calls his twelve-year-old
boy in from outside and sits him down. "This is my high
school ring. For many years I didn't wear it. It wasn't as nice
as the ones my classmates had. I was ashamed of it." There's a
catch in the father's throat.

"Now I realize that this ring was the best your grandparents
could afford. I was the first in the family to graduate high school,
and they were very proud of me. They wanted so much for me, and
the ring was a symbol of their hope and faith in me. Now I give this
ring to you."

The boy stands mute, transfixed. He and his dad know something big just happened. It will take the boy years and many pas-

sages to understand it all. But he has time.

> *My child, give me your heart, and let your eyes observe my ways.*

Proverbs 23:26

January 28   Silence

It is a cold day; there is no sun. We walk through snowy woods together, my daughter and I, absorbing the silence. On greener, sunnier days this patch of earth is filled with birdsong and insect hum and wind through rustling leaves. But today there is silence.

Beneath the snow, though, life continues. Bulbs are gathering strength and courage to erupt some months hence and toss their heads toward the sun. When we get home, there will be hearty soup and a long nap. We'll sleep so deeply that we won't remember our dreams. But they will be gathering strength and courage and scheming to bring forth new life.

> *Listen to me; be silent, and I will teach you wisdom.*

Job 33:33

January 29   Ice storm

My teenage daughter is out with the car. I go to the window and see that sleet has started to fall. I know I will not sleep until I see the car pull up in front of the house. I try to read and can't. Solitaire is no distraction. There are no good old movies tonight on television. I watch the icy rain falling, causing the trees and sidewalks and streets to sparkle like diamonds. If I knew for certain that in less than an hour my daughter would return home safe and sound, I would be enjoying nature's grand display.

No, on second thought, I would probably be sleeping right through this natural beauty. I guess even parental anxiety has an upside.

> *For you have been a refuge to the needy in their distress, shelter from the rainstorm.*
>
> **Isaiah 25:4**

January 30 — Learning to be a parent

A group of parents are waiting for ballet class to finish up. "Here's one lesson that will make your life as a parent much easier," my friend Jane explains. "Whenever the kids are going to share something, you let one cut it in half and the other choose which piece to take. That stops the bickering and teaches them fairness."

Where do we learn all this parental wisdom, I wonder.

In time I realize that outside every tap dance class and soccer practice and basketball game there's another school going on—a school for parents. God, so often when you want to take care of us you do so by sending other people into our lives. Help me to be open to this help...and give it freely to others.

> *The angel answered him, "I am Gabriel and I was sent to speak to you and tell you this good news."*
>
> **Luke 1:19**

My daughter got mad at me yesterday when I told her she had to clean up her mess. She pouted, cried and told me she didn't want me to be her father.

I do that to you, don't I, God? I throw adult versions of tantrums, in effect telling you that I don't want you to be my father.

Today, after a good night's sleep, she sidles up to me and says she's sorry. She cleans up her messes with energy and joy. I find it easy to welcome her back into my good graces. In my joy at reconciling with her, I get a glimpse of your joy when I turn back toward you.

Rejoice with me, for I have found my sheep that was lost.

Luke 15:6

February 1   "Tap and Mot"

Watching my two toddlers practice writing, I smile to see them get some of their letters and numbers backwards. I think of my older brother, Pat, who was my first friend and fiercest defender. The two of us are still teased by our aunts and uncles and cousins for long ago signing our names dyslexicly "Tap" and "Mot."

Eventually my children will learn their lessons and the letters will get put down in the correct order. But forever in my mind, the phrase "Tap and Mot" will capture the love of two brothers.

My prayer is that my two daughters will also come to know that same deep and abiding sibling friendship and that it will see them through life's passages.

> ***Whoever loves a brother or sister lives in the light, and in such a person there is no cause for stumbling.***
>
> **1 John 2:10**

February 2   In due time

In her book, *One Writer's Beginnings,* author Eudora Welty tells how the gonging, clanging and cuckooing of the many clocks in her childhood home instilled in her a strong sense of chronology. "It was one of a good many things I learned almost without knowing it; it would be there when I needed it."

I hope my kids learn about prayer that way. Their mother and I punctuate our days with prayer—upon waking, at meals, before big trips, in times of trouble. I'm hoping that the habit of prayer will be there for my children when they need it, just like Eudora Welty's sense of time.

*Rejoice always, pray without ceasing, give
thanks in all circumstances; for this is the will of
God in Christ Jesus for you.*

1 Thessalonians 5:16-18

February 3   Free gift, part 1

Have you intuitively known how to handle a tough situation in your family? That's the gift of Wisdom. The Holy Spirit has this and many other gifts in store for you. Keep an eye out for them.

*I have good advice and sound wisdom; I have
insight, I have strength.*

Proverbs 8:14

February 4   Happy Birthday, Dad

Today is my father's birthday. My gratitude for the gifts he's given me grows with each passing year.

From my earliest childhood, I can remember him rising early each morning to attend 6:30 Mass. I also remember him driving me to church on my first morning as an altar boy. From the sacristy next to the altar, I looked out before Mass began. In the sparse crowd I spied my dad—on his knees, head bowed, deep in prayer.

Every child should see the man they most admire kneeling before a power greater than us all.

*O come, let us worship and bow down, let us
kneel before the Lord our Maker!*

Psalm 95:6

February 5   Spiritual dryness

The desert holds a special place in Christian imagination. Moses led the Hebrew people through the desert to the Promised Land. God delivered manna and water in the desert. Jesus spent forty days in the desert and was tempted there.

It appears that if you take your faith seriously you will eventually wind up in a place of spiritual dryness.

But it's hard as a parent to be feeling empty while everyone else in the family is bubbling full of life. God, wherever you are, help me to hang in there today.

> *Then Jesus was led up by the Spirit into the*
> *wilderness to be tempted by the devil. He fasted*
> *forty days and forty nights, and afterwards he*
> *was famished.*
>
> **Matthew 4:1-2**

February 6   The jerk list

Okay, I'll admit it. I'm crabby today. Everybody I run into ticks me off, including the kids. After listening to my growing tale of woe, however, a friend explains his theory of the "jerk list."

He says, "If you find yourself having one of these days, make a list of everybody who has angered you. If you get to ten names, cross off the other names and put your own at the top of the list."

> *Why do you see the speck in your neighbor's eye,*
> *but do not notice the log in your own eye?*
>
> **Matthew 7:3**

February 7 The universe as puzzle, part 1

Whent my children were four and six, a package arrived from UNICEF. It was a puzzle in the shape of a circle, with a scene of outer space in the center, ringed by concentric circles of animals, landscapes, and people from all around the world holding hands. The kids put on their pajamas while my wife made popcorn and I set up the card table. We settled in for a long night of laughter and puzzle fixing.

Little did we know that putting puzzles together would become one of our family rituals for years and years.

Thank you, God, for showing up in our fun.

> *Rejoice before the Lord your God—you and your sons and your daughters.*

Deuteronomy 16:11

February 8 Our Father

Today at church the priest opened up the Prayers of the Faithful to the whole church. He handed the microphone to anyone who wanted to voice a prayer.

People came forth with heartfelt petitions about grandmothers who were sick, husbands who were undergoing terrible surgeries, sons and daughters who were struggling with alcohol or drugs, and on and on.

When the time came to say the Lord's Prayer, we all instinctively reached out and grabbed the hands of those around us. Perhaps it was the first time I actually realized the meaning of starting out with "Our Father," not "My Father."

Pray for one another, so that you may be healed. The prayer of the righteous is powerful and effective.

James 5:13-16

February 9   Drop a line

A priest friend of mine conducted what he called his "ministry of the short note." Every day he'd notice someone who was doing good work—a teacher, a social security administrator, a politician, a checkout clerk at the grocery store. He'd drop them a short note to tell them they were deeply appreciated, and he never expected them to respond.

This is also a good spiritual discipline for parents. Sometimes our kids can't stand to hear another word from us. So drop your child a short note—in their lunchbox, on their pillow, stuck in a book or backpack. Mention something you noticed about your son or daughter that made you especially proud.

And don't expect them to acknowledge the note. They will, but in their own time and perhaps not even to you directly.

And now, my children, listen to me, and be attentive to the words of my mouth.

Proverbs 7:24

February 10   When did we see you?

H ow do we learn to live as people of faith? A friend told me this story about her late father, a prominent attorney. Her dad and mom had come to visit and they all went to church at the daughter's parish. A homeless man, disheveled and dirty, had fallen asleep in the pew in front of them. Someone might have complained to the ushers, for one came and was ready to roust the man.

My friend's father put his hand on the usher's shoulder, however, and in a voice that was both quiet and powerful said, "Let him be. He is welcome here."

My friend told me, "Dad had often spoken to us about his faith, but that moment defined something for me that I will never forget."

> *When did we see you a stranger and welcome you?*
>
> **Matthew 25:38**

February 11   The Pieta

Last summer I stood in St. Peter's Church in Rome, mesmerized by Michelangelo's Pieta. His scene of a tender mother, impossibly young, vulnerable in her grief and holding the lifeless body of her son, is Michelangelo's most compelling religious lesson for all parents. In our deepest sorrows, all that is left to us is to hold our pain in our arms and await the presence of God.

> *God himself will be with them; he will wipe every tear from their eyes. Death will be no more; mourning and crying and pain will be no more.*
>
> **Revelation 21:3-4**

February 12   The inner critic

We parents can be hard on ourselves. In fact, many of us have a play-by-play announcer constantly prattling on in our heads: "Oooh, Tom blew it again! Look at how he mishandled *that* interaction with his kids."

It's time to fire the inner critic. Send him or her packing. Sure we parents make mistakes. And it's important to address those mistakes by apologizing to our children when appropriate and making amends to them when possible. But it does no good to subject ourselves to constant, cruel criticism. (You wouldn't let anyone do that to your kid, would you?)

> *You have spoken harsh words against me, says the Lord. Yet you say, "How have we spoken against you?"*
>
> **Malachi 3:13**

February 13   The challenge

The late Cardinal Joseph Bernardin issued a stirring challenge to teachers, and his words apply as well to parents. He said, "What we need now is to engage our people, to truly listen, to explain, to challenge, to show that our tradition really makes sense and, in the long run, better responds to their deepest longings and aspirations than anything else. This is our primary task. We dare not fail."

Consider the steps he suggests: to engage our children, to listen, to explain, to challenge, and to show. To do these things we need to stay close to our kids, close enough to spot the stirring of the Spirit in their hearts and in their lives.

> *A new heart I will give you, and a new spirit I will put within you; and I will remove from your body the heart of stone and give you a heart of flesh.*
>
> **Ezekiel 36:26**

February 14   Hearts full of love

I remember the forlorn feeling one Valentine's Day when I was in grammar school, waiting for a heart-shaped envelope adorned with Patty O'Rourke's perfect penmanship to land on my desk. Though children may act tough and self-sufficient, they all want to be loved.

It's tempting for us parents to try to find materialistic ways to make our kids more popular—with clothes, activities, the latest gadgets. But in the long run, the surest way they will become more lovable is when they become more loving.

Our job is to nurture their sensitivity, their self-awareness, their kindness, and their generosity. Here's a suggestion: At dinner tonight, have each person around the table offer two compliments to every other person sitting there. Such practices will prepare them for many Happy Valentine's Days to come.

> *I give you a new commandment, that you love one another. Just as I have loved you, you also should love one another.*

John 13:34

February 15   Great expectations

Try this experiment. Take a moment to breathe deeply. Now turn to the rest of your day with the gentle expectation that God will show you something wonderful and new—about yourself, about your children, about the life you are called to live.

Sometimes all we need is a new set of eyes and an expectant heart.

So if anyone is in Christ, there is a new creation;
everything old has passed away.

2 Corinthians 5:17

February 16   All the advantages

Not surprisingly, we parents want to give our children all the advantages life has to offer. And so our children have grown up with more "stuff" and more new experiences than any other generation before them. And yet the statistics about young people are troubling: a rise in addictions, eating disorders, depression and suicide.

These problems manifest themselves in the physical, but the solutions are spiritual. One advantage that we parents can give our children is a spirituality that gives meaning to their days.

There is no sure formula for passing on a living faith. But our effort to do so deserves even more attention than we give to music lessons, sports camps, or picking out a high school or college.

For by grace you have been saved through faith,
and this is not your own doing; it is the gift of
God.

Ephesians 2:8

February 17   Peas in a pod

A dad is working on his car with his son. The dad points to a part in the engine and tries to explain how it functions and how to replace it. The boy, eager and impatient, just wants to get his hands on the tools and start taking things apart.

"I know, I know," he tells his dad before the man even has time to finish his explanations. The tone in his son's voice strikes a chord within the father. It is the same one the man uses with his boss, his wife...and his kids.

The traits that irritate us in our children are the very traits we loathe in ourselves.

> *As God's chosen ones, holy and beloved, clothe yourselves with compassion, kindness, humility, meekness, and patience.*
>
> **Colossians 3:12**

February 18   Wondrous dad

I asked my grown children to recommend a meditation theme for this book from our life as a family.

"Tell about how you used to draw for us," my daughter Patti suggested.

"Huh?"

"Yeah, remember when we asked you to draw our house and it looked just like our house. We were so amazed. And when you would draw trees, they really looked like trees."

I'm very feeble at drawing, but I do remember doodling with them when they were young. Today they're both artistic and can figuratively draw circles around me. I'm glad they remember those days the way they do, though. I'm glad there was a time their daddy could do wondrous things.

> *I will call to mind the deeds of the Lord; I will remember your wonders of old.*
>
> **Psalm 77:11**

February 19   "We're home"

We're coming home late from a family gathering. Exhausted from running around with her cousins, my daughter falls asleep in the back seat of the car. As I reach in to lift her out and carry her into the house, she moans because the cold air swirls around her and she doesn't want to be disturbed.

I'm like that now, too, Lord. I get into a safe routine and don't want to be moved out of my cocoon, even though I know that staying too long in a cocoon turns it into a tomb. Help me to trust you, like my child trusts me, knowing that you are holding me close and bringing me where I need to be.

> **But I trust in you, O Lord; I say, "You are my God."**
>
> **Psalm 31:14**

February 20   Practicing real presence

In preparation for our children's First Communion, a number of families in our parish have gathered around our dining room table. We've just moved into our home, and I'm a bit embarrassed, aware of all the decorating projects in the old house that remain unfinished and the flaws in need of repair.

The parents and kids are making banners that will hang at the ends of the pews on First Communion day. We discuss meals we've had that stick in our memory, and it quickly becomes clear that what makes a meal memorable for people is not the quality of the furnishings but the connections with the people around the table.

As we continue our cutting and gluing and pasting, stopping occasionally for a bite of cookie or sip of coffee or milk, a sense of joy fills our dining room. The laughter rises and falls, people tease each other with ease and underlying kindness. A group of strangers becomes a kind of extended family around our dining room table. As I look around, I no longer focus on what's not there and begin to glimpse what is.

> *When he was at the table with them, he took*
> *bread and broke it, and gave it to them. Then*
> *their eyes were opened and they recognized him.*
>
> Luke 24:30-31

February 21   Surprise, surprise

When the kids were little and our house was small and their piles of toys grew and grew (thanks to the generosity of aunts and uncles and grandparents), my wife came up with a good idea. We put the toys in big laundry baskets and brought most of them up into the attic. Then every week we'd rotate a new basket down (putting the old one away).

It was like a mini-Christmas each week. The kids would greet old toys as if they were precious and new. Rather than taking the big pile for granted, they began to appreciate the few toys in front of them.

I'm ready for Lent to begin soon. I could benefit from having some of the "stuff" in my life removed for a time so I could appreciate it when it returns.

> *Give to everyone who begs from you; and if*
> *anyone takes away your goods, do not ask for*
> *them again.*
>
> Luke 6:30

February 22   Bringing work home

Last night I was a total crab. Unfit to live with. Snapping at everyone.

I was worried about work. Still nursing wounds from imagined slights, I kept replaying scenes from the workday and thinking about what I should have said or done.

Meanwhile the evening went by. The children went to bed. We never really connected.

I never did solve the problems from work; I only dug myself deeper into an emotional hole. I vow to try a different approach today. As I look in the mirror, I make the first important change. "God, help me keep my perspective," I say.

Then I go wake up the kids and give them a big hug.

So then, whenever we have an opportunity, let us work for the good of all, and especially for those of the family of faith.

Galatians 6:10

February 23   Always and never

You *never* let me play with my friends!"

"You *always* let him have the first piece of cake!"

"You *never* clean up your room when I ask!"

"You *always* lose your gloves!"

Absolutes in a family are rarely true—for either children or adults. In fact, speaking in absolutes like *always* and *never* is often quite damaging to the effectiveness of our communication and to the tender hearts of those with whom we're communicating.

Let your word be "Yes, yes" or "No, no"; anything more than this comes from the evil one.

Matthew 5:37

February 24 "The Wall"

My wife teaches seventh graders. She says her job is to be "the Wall."

Her theory is that children's job is to test limits. They try to wander off into all sorts of behaviors, and she's the wall they bump into that lets them know they've gone too far. If they don't hit "the Wall," they might just keep going and we'll lose them.

Parents sometimes need to be "the Wall" to their children. Too many kids are living without walls.

> *"Peace be within your walls, and security within your towers." For the sake of my relatives and friends I will say, "Peace be within you."*
> **Psalm 122:7**

February 25 Tell me a story

Tell me a story, Mommy."

"Well, there was once a little boy who had a lot of problems, even before he was born. Many people, even the doctors, said he probably wouldn't make it. But this little boy kept trying and trying, and soon he was born. But he was very, very tiny, and the doctors thought he might not live very long and would never get to run and play with his friends. But that tiny baby boy kept trying and trying and wanting to live. Day by day, he grew stronger and bigger and healthier. And that made his mommy very, very happy."

"Is that me, Mommy?"

"Yes, that's you." And she kissed the top of his head just a moment before he leapt off her lap and went off to run and play with his friends.

For it was you who formed my inward parts;
who knit me together in my mother's womb.

Psalm 139:13

February 26   Sweat the small stuff

The man's son hadn't been in preschool more than a week before he adopted an uncharacteristically sarcastic tone with his friends and siblings. It was all the rage among the preschoolers—the mark of being cool among five-year-olds.

But Dad didn't like it. He wanted his sweet and tender boy back.

At every stage a child enters, parents lose something they loved from the previous stage. Being a parent is filled with many losses. Some are large, and some are small. But they all matter.

> *Blessed be the God and Father of our Lord Jesus*
> *Christ, the Father of mercies and the God of all*
> *consolation, who consoles us in all our afflic-*
> *tion, so that we may be able to console those*
> *who are in any affliction with the consolation*
> *with which we ourselves are consoled by God.*

2 Corinthians 1:3-4

February 27   Help from our friends

A blizzard has our whole neighborhood socked in. No cars have traveled down our street all evening. Our neighbor down the block, an odd guy who keeps to himself, gets in his car and tries to pull away. He keeps revving the engine and rocking back and forth, but the car is stuck and won't budge from the curb.

The kids watch as I put on my coat and boots and gloves and

trudge over to see if I can help him. I get near his car to start pushing and he screams, "Don't touch my car! Stay away!"

"Hey, I just wanted to help."

"Get away! Get away!"

At first I feel shame, then anger. But as I watch with my children from our living room window as he continues to fruitlessly grind his gears, a huge sadness comes over me. How frightening life must be if you cannot accept the help of friends and neighbors. It is a lesson I want my children to learn.

> *How does God's love abide in anyone who has*
> *the world's goods and sees a brother or sister in*
> *need and yet refuses help?*
>
> **1 John 3:17**

February 28   Whistle while you play

At about eighteen months old, our firstborn loved *The Muppet Show*. When the first strains of its theme song came on she'd run into the family room, stand shaking in front of the television set, and almost levitate from excitement.

One time she stood there with puckered lips, breathing in and out excitedly, and suddenly she let out a loud whistle. This surprised (and pleased) her immensely, so she kept trying to do it again—with varying degrees of success.

My kids have shown me how often our talents and abilities arrive unexpectedly. It never pays to underestimate what we are capable of.

> *Now there are varieties of gifts, but the same*
> *Spirit; and there are varieties of services, but the*
> *same Lord; and the same God who activates all*
> *of them in everyone.*
>
> **1 Corinthians 12:4-6**

February 29   Frank's sneaky treats

W e're visiting friends who also love our kids. Frank calls the girls into the kitchen where he makes them special kiddy cocktails, sneaking maraschino cherries into their glasses.

"Now don't tell your Dad! He'll want to eat them all up himself," he whispers. The girls giggle and peek around the corner. I catch them out of the corner of my eye but pretend not to notice.

This is a ritual played out each time we come to Frank's house. It's his special sign of welcome and hospitality. Yet I know that it goes deeper than that. Frank's sneaky treats are also sacramental actions that reveal something about the sneakiness of God's grace.

> *Do not neglect to show hospitality to strangers,*
> *for by doing that some have entertained angels*
> *without knowing it.*
>
> **Hebrews 13:2**

March 1 — Being there

One of the best gifts we parents can give our kids is our "un-anxious" presence. This is not always easy to do, with so many distractions pulling at us and at them. But sometimes we're lucky and this kind of interaction is forced upon us.

This happened to me one day when I was with my daughter, Patti, on a ski outing with our parish youth group. We were on a ski lift, about three-quarters of the way up Cascade Mountain in Wisconsin when the lift mechanism stalled out. The sun was beginning to set, and the skiers below us cast long shadows as they swooped down the slopes. We sat in silence as we watched the skiers glide and the snow boarders swoosh, kids and adults alike smiling as they collected at the bottom of the ski runs. Large black crows circled in the distance, or perched on bare branches in the oak trees at the mountain's crest. Patti and I said few words, but what we said indicated we were in tune with the place, the moment, and with each other. As it says in those credit card commercials, the experience was "priceless."

Being present in the moment is always a choice. If we do it often enough, it can become a habit.

> *Remember I am with you always, to the end of the age.*
>
> Matthew 28:20

March 2 — What we do for love

A group of friends were sharing stories about being the parents of teenagers. One friend topped us all. On a recent shopping trip, her fourteen-year-old son asked her, "When we get into the mall, can you, like, pretend you don't know me, okay?"

Being a parent means loving them when they are two and say they hate you. It means loving them when they are six and break your antique vase. It means loving them when they are thirteen and tell you about the cool parents of their friends who "aren't so old fashioned as you." Or when they're seventeen and you get a call from the police station in the middle of the night. It surely doesn't mean enjoying all these stages or approving of all these behaviors. But we are still called to provide the best remedy to what ails them: to love them through it.

> *For the mountains may depart and the hills be removed, but my steadfast love shall not depart from you, and my covenant of peace shall not be removed, says the Lord, who has compassion on you.*

> **Isaiah 54:10**

March 3   Seekers

A lot of the adults I talk to say their own faith was greatly nurtured by what they witnessed their parents doing. For some it was saying the Rosary. For others it was reading the Bible. Some said their parents had a great devotion to a particular saint, and others saw their parents always going out of their way to help the down-and-out.

It's important to *tell* our kids what we believe. But it's always much more powerful to *show* them what we believe. Polly Berrien Berends, author of *Whole Child/Whole Parent*, says, "If they see you seeking, they will seek. The finding part is up to God."

> *Ask, and it will be given you; search, and you will find; knock and the door will be opened for you.*

> **Matthew 7:7**

March 4   Shadowboxing

A friend offered an insight about being a parent that has helped me a great deal. She said, "Every time my kids reach a new age, it triggers unfinished business inside me that was left over from when I was that age. And I can easily find myself overreacting with my kids when it's not really their issue. Rather than 'fixing' it in them, I need to deal with it inside of me."

This insight has helped me numerous times—from early on when my kids began playing organized sports (what parent has not relived their youthful triumphs and heartaches from the sidelines?), through when they began questioning authority, to their first days at a new job. When I recognize that such events unleash trapped energy in me and then deal with that first, I find I am much more able to be helpful, creative and caring to my kids in the moment, rather than shadowboxing with my past.

> *For inquire now of bygone generations, and*
> *consider what their ancestors have found; for we*
> *are but of yesterday, and we know nothing, for*
> *our days on earth are but a shadow.*
>
> **Job 8:8-9**

March 5   Being rather than doing

We were visiting friends and their kids were showing off their accomplishments and talents. Their older son had made an elaborate starship out of plastic blocks. Their older daughter played a fine piece on the piano. The younger son kept us laughing with his jokes and antics. It was nice to see such bright kids engaged in life.

Their younger daughter, however, was coming down with the flu, and all she wanted to do was sit on her daddy's lap. I vividly remember the times one of my children simply wanted to sit on my lap and be held. I would sometimes feel guilty, because despite the fact that she was feeling ill, I so enjoyed the cuddling. At times like that children don't have to accomplish or perform to bring delight.

I suspect that God might feel the same way about us—pleased with our achievements but oh so delighted when we need comforting.

> *Comfort, o comfort my people, says your God.*
>
> Isaiah 40:1

❧ ❧

March 6   Free gift, part 2

Have you stopped yourself from getting angry with your child long enough to consider what it feels like to be in his or her shoes? That's the gift of Understanding, another of the seven gifts of the Holy Spirit.

> *Whoever is slow to anger has great understanding.*
>
> Proverbs 14:29

❧ ❧

March 7   Connect the dots

After dinner the girls take out their coloring books. We're having fun coloring and talking, and they're telling me wild stories. My younger daughter asks for help with a connect-the-dots puzzle in her coloring book. This one is pretty advanced, and I'm sure she doesn't know all the numbers. As we work through it, however, she picks up on the pattern, and soon an elaborate drawing of a bird appears.

Sometimes as a parent I don't see a pattern, only confusion. But if I stay with it and do one thing at a time in some logical order, I can make sense out of situations that baffle me.

God, sometimes I need your help to connect the dots.

All things should be done decently and in order.

1 Corinthians 14:40

March 8   Sweet dreams

When I was a young child I would always worry until my parents came home. Even though I loved the older kids who babysat for us (especially my cousins), when it was time for bed I never felt totally comfortable until my parents got home. Only after they finally came into my room, kissed my forehead, and wished me sweet dreams could I sink into a trouble-free sleep.

Tonight I sit vigil at my father's side in the hospital. He's recuperating from major surgery and the painkillers have left him confused and disturbed. Last night he awoke in distress and could hardly be consoled.

And so tonight I sit with a head full of memories and a heart full of gratitude. When he wakes in turmoil, I kiss his forehead and wish him sweet dreams. It seems only fair.

Honor your father and your mother so that your
days may be long in the land that the Lord your
God is giving you.

Exodus 20:12

March 9   Steel-toed shoes

As a younger man I worked a few summers at a cemetery with the landscape crew. When I received my first paycheck, I was aggravated to see a major deduction for mandatory steel-toed shoes. What a rip-off, I thought.

I was probably still grumbling the next day when I saw sparks flying from under a tree branch I was cutting with a chain saw. The sparks were flying from where the saw blade was meeting the steel in my shoes!

I often rebel against what's good for me, especially if it's someone else's idea. I see that trait in my kids, as well. I realize that there are times when I can allow my children more choice in their lives. And there are other times—dealing with their physical or moral safety—when I need to step in and make my decision for them mandatory.

To see the wisdom of that, all I have to do is wiggle my toes.

The price of wisdom is above pearls.

Job 28:18

March 10   Grumpy Bear

The girls were young that Saturday afternoon at winter's end in Chicago. Many parents apparently had the idea that it would be good to get the kids out of the house, and so the Saturday matinee at the local movie theater was jammed with screaming kids watching a Care Bears animated feature.

After two hours of heaven for kids and hell for parents, we were streaming out. On display were loads of overpriced toys, and one poor little girl stood bawling and pointing at some item she desperately needed. Her mom, who I'm sure was normally a lovely person, had had enough. She stood screaming at her daughter (after just having seen the Care Bear movie): "I don't care! Do you understand me? I just don't care!"

My heart went out to this mom and little girl. They started out expecting one of those precious parent-child times together and wound up in tears. On the way past them I uttered a silent prayer wishing them two things: first, that they would both soon calm down, apologize to one another, and have a good Saturday evening; and second, that the Mom would soon come to recognize the hilarious irony of her protests and have a good laugh at herself.

Being a parent is much too important a task to tackle without a sense of humor.

He will yet fill your mouth with laughter.

Job 8:21

March 11   Good reception

Atelevision commercial advertising a phone service features an earnest young man, cell phone to his ear, walking through all sorts of terrain. He keeps repeating, "Can you hear me now? Good!" as he wanders further and further afield to test the seemingly inexhaustible limits of the phone service.

It's a funny commercial, partly because it captures a very human trait. We all test each other's limits and want reassurance: "Can you hear me now?"

This is especially so with teenagers. They can work so hard to make themselves appear unlovable, with spiked hair, snarls on their faces, and music designed to torture their elders. I did the same thing with long hair, anti-war rhetoric, and the Rolling Stones when I was a kid. It's as if children need to wander to the far edges of civilization and ask, "Can you love me now?"

Next time you feel children pushing you to the limits, stop to think that they might just be testing the reliability of your connection: "Can you hear me now?" they ask.

"Loud and clear!" we answer.

You must understand this, my beloved: Let everyone be quick to listen, slow to speak, slow to anger.

James 1:19

March 12   Rainbow time

The rainbows are back!" called out my wife from the kitchen. Around this time of year the sun climbs high enough in the sky to peek over our neighbor's house to the south and shine through the small Waterford bud vase that sits in our windowsill. It casts rainbows all over the room. It is a welcome relief from the drabness of winter.

Do your children know that the rainbow is a sign of God's faithfulness sent to Noah after the flood? Tell your kids the story. Encourage them to look for other signs of God's presence in nature.

> *I have set my bow in the clouds, and it shall be a sign of the covenant between me and the earth.*
>
> **Genesis 9:13**

March 13   Somebody's got a boyfriend!

The kids from down the block are taunting one of my daughters. They tease her because it's obvious she likes one of the boys from her day camp, and they are succeeding in getting under her skin.

Why is it, Lord, that youth is so vulnerable about loving someone? They hide it so well, afraid to acknowledge their love for fear that they'll be mocked and teased.

As for me, I'm sulking because I miss the days when I was the only man in my daughter's life.

> *Love bears all things, believes all things, hopes all things, endures all things.*
>
> **1 Corinthians 13:7**

March 14   I will remember you

My friend looks shaken. He's just been to visit his mother, and her Alzheimer's is getting worse. Today, she did not recognize him. What a blow to a child at any age!

My friend went home immediately and held his own kids tight, offering a hug that he hoped would last through the ages.

As a parent I cannot imagine not knowing my own children. It seems unfathomable. Our God is a mother who always remembers. Even if we should forget everything we ever knew and even who we are, God will never forget us. What a comfort that is.

> *Do not forsake me, O Lord; O my God, do not be far from me.*
>
> **Psalm 38:21**

March 15   Let's play/be church

When I was a kid we used to play "Mass." With old bed sheets for vestments and Ritz crackers for communion, we'd mimic the sacred rituals we witnessed from afar on Sundays.

But there's a more effective way for families to be church. We can recognize that we *are* the church—right in our homes—whenever we love God, pray, offer and receive forgiveness, act generously and justly, and practice hospitality. We are church when we create an atmosphere that brings out the best in our family.

Even if all else fails, we know we are church when we love one another.

> *This is my commandment, that you love one another as I have loved you.*
>
> **John 15:12**

March 16   On guard

My kids laughed when I told them that in grammar school I used to leave space on my seat beside me for my guardian angel. It was a comfort back then to know I was not facing the rigors of second grade alone.

Guardian angels are merely one more way to express the omnipresence of God's loving care, available to us always and everywhere.

Do your kids know this prayer? It's brought comfort to many a worried child over the years:

"Angel of God, my guardian dear, to whom God's love commits me here, ever this day be at my side, to light and guard, to rule and guide. Amen."

> *He will command his angels concerning you and on their hands they will bear you up so that you will not dash your foot against a stone.*
>
> **Matthew 4:6**

March 17   Irish eyes are watching

We were at a family wedding, and at the first strains of the Irish reel the women stepped to the dance floor. Four generations, at least, were represented as women by the dozen left their seats and began to step lively to the ancient tune.

This was serious women's business. They had our attention now, and the lesson began. They were not simply dancing; they were welcoming the young ones into a tradition. It was a lesson in history, pride, loyalty and values.

The various ethnic celebrations in our families pack much more power than we typically realize. When we hand on our traditions, we are giving our kids a sense of their greater identity and tying their private story to a larger, grander epic.

Let them praise his name with dancing, making melody to him with tambourine and lyre.

Psalm 149:3

March 18   Stalled out

There are times when I feel that I'm making no progress in my spiritual life as a parent. I'm not happy with the state I'm in, but can't seem to make any forward progress.

If I'm honest, I realize I'm not concentrating on the fundamentals of parenting—acts of kindness, paying attention, doing "the next right thing" in front of me. I don't put in much work, and so I don't see any results.

Trappist Father Vincent Dwyer wrote: "The winds of God's grace are always blowing; we need only make the effort to lift our sails." God, help me to make the effort.

Whatever your task, put yourselves into it, as done for the Lord.

Colossians 3:23

March 19   A good Joe

Today is the feast of Saint Joseph, revered as a worker and the earthly father of Jesus. He's the plugger, the guy in the background, the one you know you can count on to do the right thing.

I go to the park with my kids and see a number of "St. Josephs" with their kids—men who are quiet, sure of themselves, ready to help their children try a new skill on the monkey bars or push them ever higher on the swings.

A little kid falls, runs to one of the quiet men and is wrapped in his arms. The man lifts his child up easily, tends to his pain, and sends him off running to play again. Joseph, if that's your name, you are a good man.

> *An angel of the Lord appeared to him in a dream and said, "Joseph, son of David, do not be afraid to take Mary as your wife, for the child conceived in her is from the Holy Spirit. She will bear a son and you are to name him Jesus, for he will save his people from their sins."*

Matthew 1:20-21

March 20   Lenten trilogy, part 1

There are three traditional religious practices during the season of Lent. The first is prayer.

Today, let your presence to your children be your prayer. When you reach to pick up laundry, errant toys, dirty dishes or scattered CDs, lift them up as prayers to God. Practice mindfulness, being aware that every parental action can be a deep and loving prayer.

> *Call to me and I will answer you and will tell you great and hidden things that you have not known.*

Jeremiah 33:3

There are three traditional religious practices during the season of Lent. The second is fasting.

Today, fast from critical words, sniping words, painful words to your children. Forgo small-heartedness and feast on generosity. Abstain from the junk food of your distractions and worries, and taste the plain sweetness of the present moment.

> *Is not this the fast that I choose: to loose the bonds of injustice, to undo the thongs of the yoke, to let the oppressed go free, and to break every yoke?*
>
> **Isaiah 58:6**

There are three traditional religious practices during the season of Lent. The third is almsgiving.

Today give of your abundance by offering your children your time, attention, interest and wisdom. Give of yourself freely by putting aside the newspaper, the television, the cell phone, the Internet. Look each child eye-to-eye and listen heart-to-heart.

> *You received without payment; give without payment.*
>
> **Matthew 10:8**

March 23   What about me?

God, I'm having a hard time. A rival at work is enjoying a lot of success and acclaim, and I'm jealous. I don't want to seem petty and small, especially in front of my children. Yet I find myself talking about it, wanting to spread gossip and make cutting remarks to undermine my colleague's success.

I feel like the older brother in the Prodigal Son story. I am the guy who does the right thing and doesn't get noticed. Why can't I find it in my heart to feel joy in the success of others?

I certainly want my kids to do so.

> *Then the father said to him, "Son, you are always with me, and all that is mine is yours."*
>
> **Luke 15:31**

March 24   Do we hafta?

The mom was excited to get tickets to the symphony; her two boys were definitely not looking forward to it. "Do we hafta go?" they whined.

"Yes, you do," she insisted. "You don't have to like it, but you do have to be civil."

Scrubbed, pressed and polished, they were dragged to the concert hall. The boys picked up on the excitement in the audience and realized that something interesting might be about to happen. The first piece was okay, but long. The second piece began with a crash of cymbals and got more exciting by the minute. The conductor waved his baton madly, the string section moved in unison, the horns blared and the percussionists put on a magnificent show.

"Well, what did you think?" asked Mom.

"It was okay," they admitted unenthusiastically.

The mother beamed all the way home in the glow of such high

praise from her sons.

> *Sing to him, sing praises to him, tell of all his*
> *wonderful works.*

1 Chronicles 16:9

March 25   Sacraments and sandwiches

The late author Andre Dubus wrote a lot about God's real presence in the mundane elements of family life. "A sacrament is physical," he said, "and within it is God's love." Likewise, he said, "A sandwich is physical and nutritious and pleasurable, and within it is love, if someone makes it for you and gives it to you with love."

I try to remember this truth when I'm making sandwiches for my kids or picking up their toys or doing the laundry. These can be mere chores and drudgery, or they can be small signs of love and therefore become worthy pursuits. As Dubus says, such activities are "not the miracle of transubstantiation, but certainly parallel with it, moving in the same direction."

That's the direction I want to head in with my children.

> *There is a boy here who has five barley loaves*
> *and two fish. But what are they among so many*
> *people?*

John 6:9

March 26   Repeat as necessary

Sometimes I get bored with practicing my faith—same old prayers, same old rituals, same old people in the same old pews. Even the same old failings and the same old sins I commit and confess.

Then I thought of how we sing "Happy Birthday" to our children each year. Though the song remains the same, the meaning deepens because of all that has happened during the previous twelve months. During that year, new accomplishments occurred, relationships deepened, temptations were overcome, character was challenged, life unfolded.

It dawns on me that the problem is not with the practices of faith but with *how* we practice our faith. If we're not bringing real life to our faith, then no wonder we're bored.

God, help me bring my whole and real self to you.

> *So teach us to count our days so that we may*
> *gain a wise heart.*

Psalm 90:12

March 27   True pals

Thank you, God, for the friends whom I count as my partners in life, the people who I enjoy standing shoulder-to-shoulder with.

Thank you for the friends who are raising their kids alongside mine.

And thank you for the friends whose kids are older, the friends who share their hard-earned wisdom with me.

Thanks for the friends with shoulders to cry on and the ones who are ready to laugh.

Thanks for the friends I can call on when a home-repair job goes woefully wrong, the ones who are sure to have the right tool for the job or can find one that will do in a pinch.

Thanks for the friends whose values mesh with mine, who won't let me stray too far from the straight and narrow, and who call me to be my best self.

Faithful friends are a sturdy shelter: whoever
finds one has found a treasure.

Sirach 6:14

March 28   "Just because"

When she was about four, my daughter had a pretty pink dress that would swirl out as she twirled around dancing. She loved that dress. Every morning when it was time to get dressed she would want to put it on once again. She wore it until she could no longer fit her arms into it. It brought her great joy.

There's something innocent and lovely about the delight children find in favorite things. Unlike the accumulation of status symbols that we adults get into, kids love the things they love "just because."

Lord, help me regain that enthusiasm in life, to love and enjoy things "just because."

Sing for joy, O heavens, and exult, O earth!

Isaiah 49:13

March 29   Knee-jerk "no's"

I remember a time I brought my kids and their friends to a local park. I was worried about a lot of things, and it seemed every time they asked my permission to do something I told them "no" or "not now." I wouldn't let them go on the merry-go-round because the big kids were spinning it too fast. They wanted to climb a hill and I told them "not now" because I didn't want them to get dirty.

On and on it went, until finally one little boy asked me, "Why did you bring us here anyway if we can't play?"

That was the jolt I needed. I realized I had fallen into the dreaded parental trap of saying "no" as a reflex response. It was a knee-jerk reaction, and I was the jerk!

I decided it was time to counter with a big, emphatic yes. "Okay, you guys, last one up that hill is a rotten egg!" We all ran and screamed and yelled and had a great time.

(And yes, we did get dirty, but that's what washing machines are made for.)

> *Glory in his holy name. Let the hearts of those who seek the Lord rejoice.*

1 Chronicles 16:10

March 30   Put on a happy face

I remember when I hurt my foot one summer in high school. I was actually disappointed that I'd be off crutches by the time school started. I was hoping to gain everyone's sympathy as I hobbled around looking dismal.

Jesus wasn't much for looking dismal, no matter what the situation. In fact, he had a reputation as a guy who loved a good time and loved being around kids. Having a heart full of gladness seems to be a nonnegotiable part of being a follower of Jesus.

It's something I'd like to teach my children. It's something they often teach me.

> *Fathers, do not provoke your children, or they may lose heart.*

Colossians 3:21

March 31   On whose time?

S ome friends of ours have long had a good relationship with their children, who are now adults. I asked how they did it.

"We listened whenever they wanted to talk," said the mom. "The hard part was when they were teenagers. They'd just be getting revved up when we were shutting down for the night. But we always tried to be there when they came home from being out with their friends. That was the time when whoever was having a hard time would begin to open up. They'd tell us things at midnight that they'd never dare say in the light of day."

There are times when I ache for my kids to open up and tell me more. God, keep me awake until the time is right—according to them!

> *In due time Hannah conceived and bore a son.*
> *She named him Samuel, for she said, "I have*
> *asked him of the Lord."*
>
> **1 Samuel 1:20**

April 1   Family Stories

Today is my mother's birthday. Every year on her birthday her Aunt Nell (for as long as she was alive) would call Mom and describe once again what a horribly blustery day it was the day my mother was born. In her deep Irish brogue, Aunt Nell would tell in great detail how the wind was blowing and how cold it was. Her call was a family tradition.

Family stories are important. They remind us that we are special, that we are held in memory even when not held in person. We knit ourselves into a family by the small stories and rituals, kindnesses and remembrances that we offer one another. This is how families are made.

So, happy birthday, Mom. Remember what a horribly blustery day it was the day you were born?

> *The rain fell, the floods came, and the winds*
> *blew and beat on that house, but it did not fall,*
> *because it had been founded on rock.*
>
> **Matthew 7:25**

April 2   Wounds

I hate it when my kids get hurt, whether physically or emotionally. I want to rush in and protect them from every possible threat, to fight their battles for them, to lay waste to those I perceive to be their enemies.

Yet the words a very wise friend once told me continue to echo in my brain. "The worst thing you can do for children," she insisted, "is to take away their pain."

That has always sounded heretical to me, and I continue to resist the idea that I should let my kids suffer. Yet I sense the under-

lying insight is true. In my own life, it's been pain that has prompt-
ed my greatest spiritual growth. It's often pain that leads me to surrender to God's ways.

> *For I will restore health to you, and your*
> *wounds I will heal, says the Lord.*

Jeremiah 30:17

April 3   Take down

In *Report to Greco,* Nikos Kazantzakis told the story of a holy
man who wrestled with God.

Someone asked him how he possibly expected to win.

"I am hoping to lose," the man said.

God, as a parent I am constantly fighting your will for me and
for my children. I hope you know, however, that deep down I am
hoping to lose the battle. I want to surrender to your will.

In the meantime, I gain some satisfaction knowing that even
though I'm wrestling with you, we are staying mighty close.

> *Jacob was left alone; and a man (God) wrestled*
> *with him until daybreak.*

Genesis 32:24

April 4   Almost spring

It's been cold and rainy for days, but now a fresh breeze blows
into town. The sun begins to warm and dry the earth from the
long winter, and it also refreshes our souls. We throw open the

windows and doors. Kids up and down the block ride bikes and jump rope and play hopscotch.

We all know that the cold and damp will return again before summer. But our bodies and our souls know something new is just around the corner. Thank you, God, for glimpses of spring.

> **When you send forth your spirit, they are created; and you renew the face of the ground.**
>
> **Psalm 104:30**

April 5   On-the-job training

For the second weekend in a row I need to go into work to finish a big project with an unmovable deadline. "Can we come too?" ask my children. At first I resist, knowing that I won't be nearly as efficient with them underfoot. But I miss them so deeply (and feel so guilty) that I relent.

At first they are bugging me with questions and requests to accompany them to the remote part of the office where the bathroom and drinking fountain are. But in time they settle into a game in the workroom down the hall from my office. From time to time, I hear them arguing or giggling, and it warms my heart. On the way home they tell me, "We played office."

"Tell me about it," I say.

"First we filled out all these sheets of paper with numbers and words, and then we passed them to each other. Then we scribbled something on the papers and passed them back to each other. Then we stopped for a while and just talked about our favorite TV shows."

Sounds like they got the office routine down perfectly.

> **For the fruit of good labors is renowned.**
>
> **Wisdom of Solomon 3:15**

April 6   A wake, part 1

There's been a death in the family. As we arrive at the funeral home, one of my daughters says, "I'm afraid to go in there."

"What are you afraid of?"

"I'm afraid I'll say the wrong thing and make people sad."

I admit to myself that I have the same fear. I tell her, "The people are already sad, honey. And it's not bad to be sad. Here's something you can say: I'm so sorry for your loss."

I see her practicing the words as we walk in. I realize there are all sorts of lessons parents never realized we'd have to teach.

> **To comfort all who mourn; to provide for those who mourn in Zion—to give them a garland instead of ashes, the oil of gladness instead of mourning.**
>
> **Isaiah 61:2-3**

April 7   A wake, part 2

I loved my grandmother, who died when I was in eighth grade. I remember sitting with my cousin Kay and my brother Pat in a side chapel, away from the crowds. We were telling jokes and laughing when my dad walked in.

We all froze. It seemed as though we had been caught doing something terribly wrong. I had seen Dad grieving deeply for days, and I assumed our silliness would offend him. But when he saw us his face softened. He smiled. "Ma would be happy to see you kids laughing like this. She always loved to hear her grandchildren's laughter."

I breathed a sigh of relief. I also whispered a prayer of thanks to Grandma, who once again had saved the day.

A time to weep, and a time to laugh; a time to mourn, and a time to dance.

Ecclesiastes 3:4

April 8   Where do you live?

Each day of parenthood, I get the chance to choose which land I'm going to live in—the land of fear or the land of love.

In the land of fear, I see threats to my children everywhere. I feel cramped and threatened and powerless.

In the land of love, I see opportunities for them to love and be loved everywhere. I feel open and blessed and creative.

Jesus lived resolutely in the land of love, even when his followers abandoned him for the land of fear. He was faithful to his choice even unto death, and on Easter we celebrate how his love conquered all that we fear.

> *For I, the Lord your God, hold your right hand; it is I who say to you, "Do not fear, I will help you."*

Isaiah 41:13

April 9   The new driver

It is the ultimate rite of passage, not only for him but also for her. Her young son is pulling out of the driveway—alone. After months of her coaching and running commentary, he's now heading out on his own.

He's sure of himself, and that terrifies her even more. It's not that she doesn't trust him. It's just that she knows what awaits him out there—the maniac, the incompetent, the unforeseen accident, the momentary lapse of judgment.

In time, she supposes, he will pull away in the car and she will not sit frightened at the window. But not today. Today, she practices a parent's greatest spiritual task: letting go and letting God be in charge.

> ***The Lord watch between you and me, when we are absent one from the other.***
>
> **Genesis 31:49**

April 10   Worth cheering about

The girls are in a tizzy. Our living room has become the staging ground for the pom-pom squad. It's the scene of drama and tears and more than a few hurt feelings. The girls have looked forward to cheerleading for years, but now it seems everyone is mad at everyone else. I make a move to intervene as peacemaker, but my wife gives me "the look" and I shut my mouth and let things be.

Annual cheerleading tournaments have been taking place for over forty years at our parish school. The boys form basketball teams and the girls cheer them on. In recent years, a second tournament takes place that features the girls playing basketball while the boys cheer.

When we finally get to the gym, a neighbor sitting next to me in the stands shows off the program booklet from when she was a cheerleader over twenty years before. This year her daughter is co-captain of one of the squads.

"Was there this much drama and this many tears when you were doing this?" I ask.

"Of course," she replies with a wistful smile. "It was one of the best times of my life!"

I calm down and look at all the activity with new eyes. Yes, life is chaotic, painful, messy…and wonderful. Go, team!

kids' lives as well.

As playwright Stephen Dietz says, "Friendship, not technology, is the only thing capable of showing us the enormity of the world." *Faithful friends are life-saving medicine.*

Sirach 6:16

April 13   Everything is holy

I awoke early this morning to go for a run. The weatherman predicted warmth today, and I wanted to be alive in it.

As I ran down side streets in my neighborhood, I saw lights coming on in kitchens and people out on their front porch retrieving their newspapers. I knew that inside each house the kids would soon be having their cereal or fruit or Pop Tarts and the adults would stand waiting impatiently for their first cup of coffee of the day.

Behind each door another day was beginning to unfold. Dogs were waiting to be let out, cats were finding the next cozy perch on which to nap, old men were stretching to get the crick out of their backs, old women were tuning in the day's news on the radio. Moms and Dads were stretching themselves thin to cover all the bases of another busy day.

I hear birds chirping, see buds about to burst forth into new growth, watch daffodils turn their glorious heads to the sun. I'm aware of the tremendous outpouring of life and aware of where it originates. God, thank you for life. Thank you for creativity. Thank you for abundance. Thank you for spring.

The earth shall be filled with the glory of the Lord.

Numbers 14:21

April 14   A great exchange

My friend Eileen told me of a great spiritual practice that has made a big difference in her life. Like many other parents, Eileen can at times be beset with worry about her three sons or the children she encounters at the school where she works. One day she realized that her worrying wasn't helping anyone. She decided that whenever she felt the familiar gnawing of fear, she'd begin to pray for someone in her life she was worrying about.

"The change has been remarkable," said Eileen. "I'm a whole new person. I find myself going through the day praying rather than worrying. I'm not only less fearful, I'm also far more effective in how I relate to the people in my life."

Try to practice Eileen's habit of turning worry to prayer. See the difference it will make in your own life and in your relationship with your family.

> *For this child I prayed; and the Lord has granted me the petition that I made for him.*
>
> **1 Samuel 1:27**

April 15   Let there be light!

The Easter story is so very hard to comprehend, and so I look for resurrection where I can find it:

A tired dad puts down his newspaper and summons the energy to play catch with his kids.

A nervous mom finds the words to explain to her teenage son just why she finds those new CDs he bought so offensive to her as a woman.

A teenage girl lets her younger sister tag along to the movie and this time doesn't ignore her.

A young boy finds the courage to tell his friends, "No, I'm not going to tease the new kid who's different."

A couple realize they've slowly slipped into avoiding the tough conversation they need to have if their marriage is to remain alive, and they find the courage to say what needs to be said.

I look around and see plenty of evidence to confirm what theologian Walter Wink said, "Killing Jesus was like trying to destroy a dandelion seed head by blowing on it. It was like shattering a sun into a million fragments of light."

> *Open their eyes so that they may turn from*
> *darkness to light, and from the power of Satan*
> *to God.*
>
> **Acts 26:18**

April 16 Rest

I came across the scripture passage where Jesus says, "Come to me all you who labor, and I will give you rest." And so I began to wonder what kind of rest Jesus was offering to parents. Perhaps it is:

- rest from excess worry about things we cannot change;
- rest from the notion that we are not good enough parents;
- rest from negative thinking about our children;
- rest from the gnawing suspicion that our past faults and failures cannot be forgiven and absolved;
- rest from the crazy thinking that our children's happiness depends totally on us.

Jesus is offering you rest today. But he'll never force it on you. It's a gift you need open hands, mind and heart to receive.

> *Come to me, all you that are weary and are car-*
> *rying heavy burdens, and I will give you rest.*
>
> **Matthew 11:28**

April 17   Shared discoveries

I remember when my children were born. I couldn't wait until they were old enough for me to take them places and introduce them to the world. I looked forward to taking them to playgrounds, to baseball games, to water parks.

Little did I realize that they would be the ones who helped me see the world. Whenever we'd go some place, they would find treasures—maybe a shiny rock or a bird's feather that had fallen to earth. They'd point to colorful banners billowing in the wind or shiny whirligigs spinning wildly as the breezes blew.

We would go for a walk and it would take us an hour just to make it down our own block. I'd passed that way daily for years and never really noticed anything. With them I saw the flowers and the lawn ornaments, the kitty sitting in the upstairs window, and the kind eyes of the old man who sat on his porch and watered the lawn.

> *The wolf shall live with the lamb, the leopard*
> *shall lie down with the kid, the calf and the lion*
> *and the fatling together, and a little child shall*
> *lead them.*
>
> **Isaiah 11:6**

April 18   Forgiveness

I spoke in haste and in anger. My words were cutting and harsh. I felt pain, and so I inflicted pain in return. And now I sit in even more pain, realizing how I've hurt the ones I love.

Though I've apologized, the sting of my sin remains. It will take time for me to make amends.

One question remains, Lord. Will I accept your tender offer of forgiveness? I feel I am not worthy, but who among us is ever worthy of forgiveness? That's what makes forgiveness the miracle that it is.

> *Be angry but do not sin; do not let the sun go*
> *down on your anger.*

Ephesians 4:26

April 19   Prayer before a test

I'm worried about my test tomorrow, Daddy."

"Well, let's say a little prayer that God will help you."

"Will God tell me the answers I don't know?"

"No, silly. You still have to study."

"So why should I pray?"

"You pray so you will know that God is with you, and when you are confident of that you will always do better than if you're trying to do stuff on your own."

"Even tests?"

"Especially tests. Tests of every kind."

> *Our God whom we serve is able to deliver us*
> *from the furnace of blazing fire.*

Daniel 3:17

April 20   Altar girl

With folded hands and serious face, you perform your new duties assisting at Mass. You light the candles, carry the cross, attend the reading of the sacred Scriptures, receive the gifts of the faithful.

As the sacred mysteries draw to a close, the priest invokes the words, "Let us pray." You bear the book of ancient rituals to him.

In your hands it seems light as feathers, and because of you I hear the reading of it as though it is being read to me for the very first time.

> *Then I will go to the altar of God, to God my*
> *exceeding joy; and I will praise you with the*
> *harp, O God, my God.*

Psalm 43:4

April 21   Word choice

L anguage reveals a lot about our views of parenting. Watch out for words that put a heavy burden on you and your children, words like "should," "must," "always," "never," "ought."

Usually these words are used in illogical, distorted, exaggerated ways. Life is complicated and complex, and few things are "always" or "never" the case. "Should," "ought" and "must" undermine your own authority and can put you at odds with yourself. Use the language of choice, not the language of absolutes, and you will find yourself less at war with your children.

This may seem pedantic, but try it. You'll come to know how words pack power to shape your children's lives.

> *Anxiety weighs down the human heart, but a*
> *good word cheers it up.*

Proverbs 12:25

April 22   The spanking

I t had been a long day visiting relatives. The kids were wound up and cranky. There had been no relaxation all weekend.

My wife and I simply wanted to watch a Sunday evening

movie, but the kids kept bickering relentlessly. Even when we sent them to bed early they wouldn't settle down and continued their whining and fighting and crying. The movie was about to start when they erupted again. So did I. I went into their bedroom and for the first and only time I spanked them.

Years later, I suppose there might be some ironic humor in the situation, but even now it hurts to remember. The movie, you see, was *Gandhi*, the story of a man who taught the world the value of nonviolence.

I sat and watched and swallowed bitter tears.

Peace to this house!

Luke 10:5

April 23   Bicycle built for two

I put the child safety seat on the back of my bike and we rode out to see the world. You sat there placid as a queen, taking in all her royal lands and subjects. We rode around city parks watching softball games and kids on swings. We stopped for an ice cream cone, and your eyes lit up when I handed you a rainbow sherbet.

But we strayed too long and a brisk, cool breeze began to blow from the north. As I quickly pedaled toward home, you found a snuggly spot. You pulled my shirt up over your head and nuzzled there, your cheek against my back. We must have been a curious sight to passing motorists.

All the way home my prayer was that no matter what happened in years to come you would always find a warm and safe haven in me.

God is our refuge and strength, a very present help in trouble.

Psalm 46:1

April 24   A vine idea

My wife sits in the gold chair, nursing our newborn daughter. It's a picture of serene loveliness. Absorbed with each other, they don't even notice I am watching.

At church today we sang the hymn where Jesus says, "I am the vine, you are the branches. Remain in me, you shall be fruitful." I thought about the relationship of the vine to the branches: It's hard to tell where the vine leaves off and the branch begins. The most salient characteristic of the relationship is how life flows from the vine outward to the branches to support the new life that is budding there.

Today, in a new and deep way, I understand the image of God as mother.

> *I am the vine, you are the branches. Those who*
> *abide in me and I in them bear much fruit.*
>
> **John 15:5**

~ ~

April 25   R-e-s-p-e-c-t

We didn't have a lot of rules in our house as the children were growing up (though they might disagree with that assessment). But there has always been one transgression we would not abide, and that was when any of us showed a lack of respect for another.

And so we frowned on the use of words like "dork," "stupid" and "idiot." We tried to teach our kids the tricky skill of being angry with another without losing respect for him or her.

This rule has paid off. Our children have respect for each other, for their parents, and for others. In a way, respect is the foundation of all morality. It's a deeper look into the soul that reveals each person's worth, just for being who he or she is.

You must not be partial in judging; hear out the small and the great alike.

Deuteronomy 1:17

April 26   Hope for the best

When my older daughter, Judy, was about two and a half, her mother and I were discussing a difficult family problem. We were obviously somewhat anxious, and Judy offered a response that tickled me then and has stayed with me ever since. She sweetly smiled and blurted, "Hope for the best."

I know she probably heard this phrase from my wife, but it also seemed to come unprompted from her soul. And it's a phrase I try to live by. If you want to feel depressed and defeated, the world offers plenty of ammunition for your cause. But our faith offers another outcome and another choice: "Hope for the best." Why not?

For in hope we were saved.

Romans 8:24

April 27   Sabbath

It's a common refrain among parents: We're too busy. The Judeo-Christian faith tradition, however, has a remedy for this malady, and it's not to simply work harder. The remedy is to "keep holy the Sabbath."

The Sabbath is a day set aside by God for rest and worship. It's not a day to cram all sorts of chores or leisure pursuits into, nor is it a day to simply "veg out" in front of the television set. Observing the Sabbath recognizes that we are more than our work, more than our amusements, more than any one dimension of ourselves. The Sabbath invites us to slow down enough so we might arrive at a new awareness of our own depth.

As the speed of life increases, it is a counter-cultural act of courage and faith to practice the Sabbath—with music, games and reading, with leisurely shared meals (which everyone helps prepare and clean up), and with a newfound sense of our holiness. If you want to be a "parent on purpose," find ways to practice the Sabbath with your family, beginning with formal worship, with rest, with recreation that restores rather than depletes yourself, your family, and the world.

So the people rested on the seventh day.
Exodus 16:30

April 28   Shining people

Thomas Merton, the great contemplative monk, had a remarkable experience in which he saw people "shining like the sun." It was a mystical experience where he saw people's true nature as glorious and golden children of God.

I once stood on the spot in Louisville, Kentucky, where this clarity of vision happened to Merton. It's in a downtown shopping district. When I looked around at everyone, however, they still looked like ordinary shoppers to me.

But there are times when I've seen my children shine like the sun—moments when they were out in the backyard playing, or getting ready for prom, or intently reading a great book, or sleeping like angels. And so I have a sense of what Merton saw.

Look to him, and be radiant; so your faces shall never be ashamed.

Psalm 34:5

April 29   Who are you?

On Saturday we celebrated my niece Mary Kate's First Communion. It was a wonderful occasion in so many ways. Mary Kate looked precious and earnest and innocent, as did her whole class of First Communicants. Actions speak louder than words and on that glorious day (despite the clouds and rain) these budding believers were engaged in actions designed to teach them fundamental lessons about their deepest identity. While the rest of the world wants to tell them that they are merely consumers of "stuff," the faith community of St. Walter's showed them that they are not only called to receive but to actually become the body of Christ and bread for the world.

At Communion time, we sang a litany in which the name of each new communicant was called out followed by the chanted response, "Come to the table." They learned that God is calling them by name. Then a choir of sweet and tiny voices sang the refrain: *I myself am the bread of life. You and I are the bread of life. Taken and blessed, broken and shared by Christ that the world might live.*

What a gift that at such a tender age these children were given clues to those very human questions, "Who am I and why am I here?"

> *I am the living bread that came down from heaven. Whoever eats of this bread will live forever; and the bread that I will give for the life of the world is my flesh.*

John 6:51

86

There are people who live down the block from us who have an elaborate backyard patio set. Each spring they drag it out, clean it and paint it. Throughout the summer they keep it washed and dusted. However, we rarely see them actually use it!

Farther down the block, we have some other neighbors who don't have a matched set of much of anything. Yet they seem to enjoy the weekends and afternoons and evenings in their yard. They set up rickety card tables and wobbly lawn chairs. They plop themselves down on hammocks, porch stairs or even the ground. Relatives and friends come from miles around to join them. Laughter emanates from their backyard all summer long.

There are people in this world who get ready for life and others who spend their time living it. Our kids are learning the difference merely by observing our neighbors.

> *Do not look on his appearance...but look on the heart.*
>
> **1 Samuel 16:7**

May 1 — A priceless gift

I take the train to work every day, and the ticket has a holographic emblem on it. When my children were small and intrigued by the whole idea of trains I would make a small gesture of presenting my used-up commuter ticket to one of them each month. This little "rite of passage," such as it is, has been conducted after each ticket expires: month-in, month-out, year-in, year-out. It seemed a silly practice at first, a tiny token to amuse them, but it became a tradition between us.

Even after they went away to college I would tuck a spent ticket in a letter or leave it on a pillow awaiting their return. Over time, I realized that my gift to them was not the ticket with its ghostly hologram but the daily journeys these tickets represent—journeys I took to make a living and provide for my family…and to do my part to make the world a little better place for them and everyone else.

Winter and summer, spring and fall, to work and back—I gave them the gift of stability, of conscientiousness, of "you can count on me." Surely it is not my only gift to them, but it is one I never dreamt—in my younger, wilder days—I would be able to offer.

Not one word has failed of all his good promise.
1 Kings 8:56

May 2 — Religion finds a home

I once heard a rabbi give a talk about the importance of family in keeping the Jewish faith alive, and his lesson has stayed with me regarding my own Christian tradition. He said that when the Jewish temple was destroyed around 70 AD, responsibility for much of the practice of the faith was transferred to families. The destruction of the temple was indeed a sad and sobering event, he said, but it did not mean the end of religious training and practice. It simply called families to take a larger role.

In ordinary times as well as in times of crisis, our children need to experience church as nurturing, present and real in their lives. The great news is that there is nothing stopping us parents from providing that experience of faith right in the home. No matter what crises might befall the larger church, let's not deny our children what they need most—an opportunity to come to know God right where they live.

> *For I desire steadfast love and not sacrifice, the*
> *knowledge of God rather than burnt offerings.*
>
> **Hosea 6:6**

May 3   "Man run"

While out for a Saturday morning run I crossed paths with a dad pushing his eighteen-month-old daughter in a stroller. The dad still looked a bit sleepy, but he was carrying on a conversation with his daughter, who sat up bright and wide-eyed, taking everything in. He was pointing out flowers and squirrels and doggies and airplanes, and she was looking around in such a way that you could see the wheels spinning in her head, processing every new discovery.

She stared at me as I jogged past them. A bit later I circled back, and ahead of me there they were again—the dad now sitting on a bench sipping his morning coffee and the daughter still alert and babbling. Her eyes lit up when she saw me coming. "Man run," she said, pointing at me.

It dawned on me then that I had become part of her new world. Like one of the biblical lilies of the field, I felt purposeful and good just for being the guy running past her observant view.

Consider the lilies of the field, how they grow;
they neither toil nor spin, yet I tell you even
Solomon in all his glory was not clothed like one
of these.

Matthew 6:28-29

May 4   Shame

Her son was distraught but wouldn't talk. She brushed his hair back and said, "Let me tell you something about shame. Shame is an uncomfortable feeling you get when a boundary is crossed. We all have internal boundaries that protect us. They define good behavior from bad behavior. They let us know when we're acting right and when we're acting wrong. They also let us know when others are acting wrong toward us—for that can make us feel ashamed too."

He listened.

"When you feel shame," she told him, "it provides an important opportunity. You get the chance to check out what's happening in your life—either what you're doing or what's being done to you—and you can then make a change. Sometimes you need to change your behavior, sometimes you need to confront what someone else is doing to you, and sometimes you just need to move the boundaries that are causing the problem."

He nodded.

"And remember," she said, "you don't have to handle shame all alone. There are people who love you and want to help."

He hugged.

Come, let us go up to the mountain of the Lord,
that he may teach us his ways and that we may
walk in his paths.

Micah 4:2

May 5 "The we of me"

W hen I was a teenager I attended a conference called the Summer School of the Christian Apostolate. Thousands of teens from all over the country converged on Chicago's Conrad Hilton Hotel. We were treated to inspiring workshops, insightful keynote speeches, wonderful liturgies, and lots and lots of fun. It was the 1960s, and we believed we could (and would) cure all of society's ills in our lifetime.

The lesson from one of the workshops stays with me to this day, however. It was led by two young adults—Michelle Manzione and a guy whose name I can no longer recall. (Guess which one I had the crush on.) The workshop was called "The We of Me," and we examined the many ways we are shaped and formed by key people in our lives. I was struck by how tender my fellow teenagers felt about the adults who had helped them grow up, who had guided them in some way and showed them simple human care.

Stop a minute today to think about the people who are part of the "we" of you. Say a prayer of thanksgiving for those people who contributed positively to the person you've become over time: the parents, teachers, coaches, bosses, neighbors, relatives, friends and so on. And know also that you are part of the "we" of others— your kids, for example, or the children of others—whenever you play a significant role in their lives.

We tend to think we're separate and distant from one another, but we're really all connected. I think I'll be forever grateful that at the age of seventeen I got a glimpse of that truth. To Michelle Manzione and good old what's-his-name, thank you very, very much. You guys, too, are a permanent part of the "we" of me.

So then you are no longer strangers and aliens,
but you are citizens with the saints...built to-
gether spiritually into a dwelling place for God.
Ephesians 2:19-22

May 6   The tough punk

I'm walking down a dark street alone and a young punk is swaggering toward me. He's wearing a leather jacket with all sorts of metal braids and chains on it. His eyebrows sport multiple piercings, and an angry tattoo flashes across his neck. He scowls menacingly.

I decide to try a little experiment. (Sometimes it works, sometimes it doesn't.) I look him in the eyes, smile, and say, "Hi."

This time it works. In a transformation worthy of the magician David Copperfield, the "gangsta's" face softens and smiles. I get a glimpse of what his mother must see when she looks at him—or what God sees when he looks at any of us. He looks up, a boyish grin on his face, and answers my greeting with a mumbled, "Hey, how ya doin?"

For a minute, this chastened adult remembers how painful it can be as a teenage boy in the world today.

> *If there is among you anyone in need...do not be hard hearted.... You should rather open your hand willingly, lending enough to meet the need, whatever it may be.*
>
> **Deuteronomy 15:7-8**

May 7   Juggling act

My flight has been canceled. I won't be home for my daughter's last volleyball game of the season.

Jesus warned against serving two masters, but what about juggling multiple obligations that are all good? This business trip was necessary. I owe it to my company to do my job well.

And yet I owe it to my children to be present in their lives. Sometimes the two obligations collide.

Maybe the answer is to try to live graciously in the midst of conflicting responsibilities.

Jesus, help me to juggle well.

Do what seems good to you.

1 Samuel 14:40

May 8   Culture war

Popular culture is part of life. When our kids are little, they tell the same knock-knock joke they heard at preschool over and over. A little later, they want to wear the same shirt or dress every day to school. In time, they pick up phrases ("Don't have a cow, man") that are popular with other kids. As teens they hum popular alternative rock songs as they do their homework.

Religious culture has a similar effect. Say grace every night before dinner, and pretty soon you can't eat without at least thinking about it. Wake up on Sunday and go to church, and eventually you come home humming hymns of praise. Give some change to homeless people you encounter and you'll find yourself more generous with everyone.

We need to give our children at least a fighting chance in the culture war.

You come to me with sword and spear and javelin; but I come to you in the name of the Lord of hosts.

1 Samuel 17:45

May 9   I bow to you

A friend of mine rarely gets flustered. He seems at peace no matter how difficult the situation is. I asked him how he does it.

"I bow to others," he said. "I don't do it obviously, but whenever I come into contact with someone during the day I make a point of bowing inwardly to them as a sign of my respect and an acknowledgment of the presence of God inside them. It helps me remove the fear from situations and also helps me find the love."

After he told me this, I tried to put this small but significant discipline into practice. When I remember to "bow" to others, it makes a world of difference. I try to do it especially when I'm in a situation where I'm afraid or aggravated. I try it with my kids, their friends, my coworkers, the people at my parish, and anyone who drive me nuts.

So now I do a lot of bowing, but the effort is worth the result. And so I bow to you, dear reader.

Honor everyone.

1 Peter 2:17

May 10   Doubting Tom

H ave you ever felt frustrated looking at an optical illusion because you just couldn't see what everyone else was seeing—e.g. the beautiful woman instead of the hag, the goblet instead of two silhouetted faces, or the name "Jesus" spelled out in the incomprehensible squiggles? That's how the apostle known as Thomas must have been feeling in the upper room before Jesus appeared to him directly.

Being a Thomas and having had my own share of doubts, I've always paid close attention to this scripture story. Thomas stands for all of us who have a tendency to say, "I'll believe it when I see it." At first, he just couldn't "see" that Jesus had triumphed over death and was alive and present. The question for us is how we can come to see that Jesus is alive and present in our own lives—and in the lives of our families.

That takes new, expectant, hopeful eyes of faith. We can look at parenting and see a lot of annoyances, tiresome chores and draining moments. Or we can look at the same circumstance and see opportunities to love, be loved and give life.

Unless I see the mark of the nails in his hands,
and put my finger in the mark of the nails and
my hand in his side, I will not believe.

John 20:25

May 11   Free gift, part 3

Have you clearly and firmly stated your beliefs about right and wrong to someone in your family? That's Counsel, one more gift of the Holy Spirit.

Teach them to your children, talking about them
when you are at home and when you are away,
when you lie down and when you rise.

Deuteronomy 11:19

May 12   Unfair

That's not fair!" is a cry heard from kids on every block, in every city, town or village. I'm sure that in your role of parent you've heard this phrase used against you too.

This is actually good news. A passionate sense of fairness is an essential building block in living a moral life. In fact, as the world gets further divided into extremes of "haves" and "have-nots" a desire for fairness may be the only thing that ends up saving civilization.

Nurture your children's sense of fairness, and give them the tools to use when they confront an unfair situation at play, at school, in sports, in the family. We all want a peaceful future for our children and grandchildren. Remember Pope Paul VI's ringing words of wisdom: "If you want peace, work for justice."

> *Speak out, judge righteously, defend the right of the poor and needy.*
>
> **Proverbs 31:9**

May 13   Heavenly hosts

O nce, in the midst of my bout with measles as a kid, I awoke from a feverish sleep to see a woman from our parish standing over me. My mother had an unavoidable errand to do and this kind woman had offered to watch over me for the short time Mom would be away. In my fevered state I thought the woman was an angel. In fact, she was.

In raising children we rely on many people to lend a hand. At this time of year when we honor mothers, spend a moment in gratitude not only for your birth mother but also for all the women who were "angels" in your life. You might even take a moment to write a quick note, make a short call, or say a little prayer of thanks.

And next time you feel guilty asking a friend for help in tending to your kids, remember how rich your own life becomes when you welcome such acts of kindness.

> *And suddenly angels came and waited on him.*
>
> **Matthew 4:11**

When we were young, my older brother and I loved to pore through the big, thick family bible. We weren't pious kids looking for inspiring scriptures. We were searching out the color renditions of Samson ripping the fierce lion's jaw apart or David getting ready to bonk Goliath on the bean. (Later on as a teenager, I might even have sneaked a few peeks at The Song of Songs to read about breasts being like frisky fawns!)

This kind of Bible "study" sounds irreverent and even sacrilegious, I know, but don't be so quick to knock it.

Sociologist Robert Wuthnow asked people who consider themselves religious to name what most influenced the development of their faith. Mostly, they pointed to times where "specific, deliberate religious activities were firmly intertwined with the daily habits of family routines." One that was often mentioned was the presence of religious objects—such as a family bible or religious picture—in the home.

Our kids learn what's important to us. Are there signs of your faith present in your household?

> *They shall ask the way to Zion, with faces*
> *turned toward it, and they shall come and join*
> *themselves to the Lord.*
>
> **Jeremiah 50:5**

The man found it easy to offer his son advice. And if he were honest he'd admit that the advice always had a tinge of "I told you so" associated with it.

But one day the man heard a familiar echo in his words. It was the sound of his own father, who always couched his advice in ways that made the father look good at the expense of the son.

The man was shocked into sadness. "I swore I would never do that to my boy," he said to himself.

And so the man began a new path. "From now on, son, I'll stop trying to show you how smart I am and simply be there with you as you discover your own answers."

Though the kid merely shrugged, inside his heart he was leaping cartwheels and yelling, "Hooray!"

> *The Lord our God be with us, as he was with our ancestors.*
>
> 1 Kings 8:57

May 16   Give freely

My friend is an artist and one of the most creative people I know. When my daughter, Judy, exhibited an interest in art, he was quick to encourage her. He saw her budding talent and took it seriously. Recently, when facing a creative challenge, Judy quoted words of encouragement my artist friend had told her years before.

We parents can be fonts of creativity and encouragement for children—our own and those of others. The more we give, the more we will have at our disposal.

> *Some give freely, yet grow all the richer; others withhold what is due and only suffer want.*
>
> Proverbs 11:24-25

May 17　　　　　　　　　　　　　Night watch

My dad had serious surgery, and the anesthetic and the painkillers had him dazed and confused the first few days of recovery. He had the most trouble at night, when the hallucinations seemed to take a menacing turn. I spent a couple of nights at his bedside, reassuring him that all was well, reminding him where he was, and relating all that had just happened to him. I had the chance to simply sit and hold my father's hand. It helped him find the comfort to sleep, however fitfully, and gave his body a chance to heal.

I regret all Dad had to go through, yet I am also grateful to have had the opportunity to repay him for all the times he was there to comfort and reassure me. I was blessed with the opportunity to show my father love.

When's the last time you just sat with one of your parents or an aging relative or friend? Isn't that what you hope your own children will do with you?

> *My child, help your father in his old age, and do not grieve him as long as he lives.*
>
> **Sirach 3:12**

May 18　　　　　　　　　Undercover operation

In my neighbor's yard, tulips are in bloom. Swaying in the gentle breeze, their bright splashes of color enchant all passersby.

I remember last fall when my neighbor was on her knees, planting the bulbs and mixing in food for them. For months, the bulbs lay fallow, covered in dirt and bone meal and mulch, but today it's clear that—unbeknownst to those of us who passed by—

May 20   Safe at home

We head out for the first family picnic of the season, but it's a dud. The picnic grounds are muddy; we forget the hamburger buns; the charcoal takes forever to light; the kids are too old to play on the playground equipment. Bickering begins. We call it a day early.

On the way home, I'm doing a slow burn that things didn't turn out the way I'd planned. Then I remember what a friend calls her basic rules for a "successful enough" family outing: You got there; you got back; and everyone survived. All of a sudden I'm chuckling to myself.

The kids ask, "What are you smiling about, Dad?"

I tell them, "All I can think of is, thank God *that's* over!"

We all have a good laugh. Not a bad family outing after all!

> *Suffering produces endurance, endurance produces character, and character produces hope, and hope does not disappoint.*
>
> **Romans 5:3-4**

May 21   Body and soul

In Jesus, God took on a human body. This is one of the greatest revelations in Christian belief.

Sometimes, however, our religion gets portrayed as anti-body or overemphasizes the lofty life of the spirit. Yet it's only through our body that we come to perceive the presence of God in our world. Our bodies contain a lot of wisdom if only we attune ourselves to pay attention.

Where is *your* tension? Where are you holding *your* fear? Where are you keeping *your* anger? Where in *your* body do loss and grief reside? Pay attention to your body throughout the day and it will help you find healthy ways to deal with the emotions, fears and longings that might otherwise go untended.

Help your children to become attuned to what their bodies are telling them. They will be better able to navigate life if they are united in body and soul.

> *Do you know that your body is a temple of the*
> *Holy Spirit within you, which you have from*
> *God?*
>
> **1 Corinthians 6:19**

May 22   Star witness

One of the best lessons my daughters ever received about their religion was the afternoon they snuck into Aunt Marie's room. Their great-aunt was busy at prayer, and she eagerly invited them to sit on the bed with her, one on either side. They watched bright-eyed as she paged through her well-worn prayer book. Holy cards were tucked in almost every page. She led the girls through her daily prayer routine, which included prayers for sick neighbors and friends, prayers for relatives both living and dead, and prayers for "those poor souls most in need of prayers who have no one to pray for them."

She handed each of the girls several bright and enticing holy cards and told them what they were for: "This one commemorates your great-grandmother's death. She was a great woman. A strong woman." The lessons went on and the girls were held in rapt attention.

To pass a living faith to the next generation we don't need preachers—we need witnesses.

> *And I tell you, everyone who acknowledges me*
> *before others, the Son of Man will acknowledge*
> *before the angels of God.*
>
> **Luke 12:8**

May 23   Telling the tale

When it gets to the part of Mass where the priest says, "Father, accept this offering from your whole family," I often think of our refrigerator. As our kids were growing up, the refrigerator was always adorned with drawings our kids had made or test papers with "100%" written boldly in red across the top. It would also be the repository for the flight and hotel information for my next business trip and the calling tree for my wife's school.

When the Prayers of the Faithful begin, I think of the pictures on our refrigerator of newborn nieces and nephews, the young girl we sponsor who lives in a mountain village in Guatemala, the wedding invitations and graduation announcements that are always there waiting to be RSVPed.

In many homes, the family refrigerator says more about the values and beliefs and life of the family than any other place in the home. It stands as a silent witness to our cares, concerns, values and deepest beliefs.

And you thought it was simply the machine that kept the orange juice cold.

Thus you will know them by their fruits.
                                  Matthew 7:20

May 24   What you want

All day long our kids are assaulted by artfully crafted messages telling them they deserve to have their every whim and desire immediately met: "Buy this; use that; wear this; drink that if you want to be happy."

And yet at a men's group meeting I hear someone I admire say,

"I've come to believe the old saying that happiness does not come from having what you want but from wanting what you have." That night I come home and for the first time in a long time look at what I have—a home, a family, a community of people I love. A sense of satisfaction overtakes me.

I sit and wonder how I can introduce this message to my kids in ways they might believe.

> *I have learned to be content with whatever I have.*
>
> **Philippians 4:11**

May 25   A lesson learned

My younger daughter, Patti, brought mice home from school. Her second grade teacher chose her to bring home the class mice to take care of for the summer, but they're not getting along. Gus-Gus keeps attacking Mopsy.

The best advice we get is to set them free in a field, although none of us is sure what exactly to tell the teacher next September.

Patti sits in the front seat of the car with the cage on her lap, whispering her goodbyes and offering the rodents advice on how to survive in "the wild." We wander through the woods until Patti finds just the right spot—a new home for her charges. She sets out food and water to get them off to a good start. And then it's time to open the cage.

From this experience, my daughter learned a harsh lesson about how caring sometimes leads to letting go. I learned a welcome lesson about the love in the heart of my child.

> *He reveals deep and hidden things. He knows what is in the darkness and light dwells with him.*
>
> **Daniel 12:22**

May 26   Seeing eye-to-eye

I got a great piece of parenting advice from a primary school teacher. I asked her how she kept all the kids focused and in line. She told me her secret—get on the level with them. She makes a point of connecting with kids by scrunching down and looking at them eye-to-eye while she's talking to them.

So if you feel your child (of whatever age) isn't listening or paying attention, try stopping what you're doing and establishing eye contact first. It will make a tremendous difference in how well they'll hear and listen to what you say. Besides, looking into those eyes will remind you just how beautiful that child of yours truly is.

> *We look not at what can be seen, but at what cannot be seen; for what can be seen is temporary, but what cannot be seen is eternal.*
>
> **2 Corinthians 4:18**

May 27   Care of the sole

I know a guy who is willing to give his running shoes time to restore themselves, but he doesn't offer himself the same consideration. He read somewhere that it's wise to give your running shoes a chance to "rebound" and regain their original cushiness and shape after a long run. And so he gives his shoes some time off after every major effort.

Yet this guy drives his body and mind relentlessly day after day. Even his rest and relaxation involve getting things done or straining for some goal.

Maybe this works for him, but I think his running shoes get the better end of the deal. I know for myself that I have to build in some restoration times for myself. I need down time after major projects, long days, tough patches when my kids are going through hard times, or simply when a number of family and work commitments fall together and there's more to do than there is day to do it in.

I find that prayer can help. It can be a time that really restores because it includes time for my soul. This is true of morning or evening quiet time alone, but it is especially so of Sunday worship when I can get "lost" in prayer. And when I'm even too tired to actively pray I feel carried along by the more energetic members of the congregation around me. I usually come out feeling at least a little restored and better balanced.

> **My presence will go with you, and I will give you rest.**
>
> Exodus 33:14

May 28   Remember

Back when I was teaching high school I spent my summers working for the Catholic Cemeteries of Chicago. I was on a crew of guys who trimmed trees, laid sod and planted flowers. Our focus was on new life. We worked on what was going to grow tomorrow, not what had died yesterday.

Yet every day we encountered many people who were paying mind to yesterday and honoring memory. We'd see a widow or widower passing the day on a folding chair set up next to a grave. We'd observe flags adorning the graves of fallen soldiers and stuffed animals and pinwheels on the tiny graves of children. We'd watch as whole families enjoyed a picnic near the grave of their grandmother. Throughout the day people would stop in to spend a few minutes at a grave, to trim the grass away from a headstone, or to place flowers on a grave.

At first I found this living in the past to be morbid. But I came to appreciate mourning as a holy practice, an honoring of a reality our society is often quick to dismiss: Present to us is "a cloud of witnesses"—holy men and women who have gone before us and left us the legacy of the gospel of their lives.

Modern life, even with all its freedoms and choices, can seem empty and lonely. At the heart of our faith is a simple invitation to remember. Help your kids develop this capacity. A good memory can help them discover who they really are.

> *Take care, so as neither to forget the things that your eyes have seen nor to let them slip from your mind all the days of your life; make them known to your children and your children's children—how you once stood before the Lord your God.*

Deuteronomy 4:9

May 29   ABC Zones

At the start of every summer my children and I would have to review the rules again: What time is curfew? Why do you need to call if you won't be home on time for dinner? How far can you stray from home without permission?

The kids still laugh at my elaborate scheme to set up "zones." Zone A was our block up to the Guidi's house. Zone B was anything passed that to Grace Street and over to Addison. Zone C ("You can't go there without permission") was anything up to the Six Corners shopping area.

Years later, on the night before my daughter was heading off to a year of study in Ecuador, she turned and asked, "Would this be Zone Z, Dad?"

'Yes, it would,' I think to myself amidst the general laughter, 'and I've been preparing us for it all your lives!'

> *Train children in the right way and when old they will not stray.*

Proverbs 22:6

May 30   Surprise!

C'mere and watch this," whispers my wife to me on a day I was working at home. We stand in the doorway to the living room where our two daughters are playing. They hear the first strains of the theme song from "Mr. Rogers Neighborhood" on the television and drop their toys and scurry to the hallway. This has become a daily ritual. They hide, giggling around the corner where the TV can't see them, and when Mr. Rogers comes into his house, hangs up his jacket, changes his shoes, and stands to greet the boys and girls, my daughters jump out from their hiding place to surprise him.

And with his welcome smile, Mr. Rogers let's them know he's always glad to see them.

> ***Greet one another with a kiss of love.***
> **1 Peter 5:14**

May 31   Parish festival

The kids have been waiting for this day. We all have. Each year at the beginning of summer our parish holds a festival with rides, games and live entertainment. The kids love it because they get to run around freely with all their friends. We parents enjoy it because we know our kids are safe within the confines of the parish grounds. We all know that lots of co-parishioners will keep an eye on all the kids as they run and chase and have a good time.

The big tent reminds me of the church: There's plenty of room for plenty of people; we're all needy; we all have our gifts as well as our foibles; and magic happens when we gather together to tell stories and enjoy the feast. Toward the end of the night the band is hitting its stride. The music is loud and the beat is strong. Everyone is up off their seats: the young and the old, the conservative and the liberal, people who would normally not be under the same roof. We're all shaking our tail feathers and waving our arms above our heads.

Something emerges from deep inside me: "Thank you, Jesus!"

> *And the streets of the city shall be full of boys*
> *and girls playing.*

Zechariah 8:5

June 1   Free yourself

S omeone mentioned the name of a person from my past who, in my mind, had done me wrong. I found myself as angry and agitated as if the offense had happened that day rather than decades ago. I talked this over with a friend I trust. He said, "I'll bet you wish you had all that energy available to use for other things."

I didn't really want to hear that, but I had to agree. As delicious as it is to feel righteously angry, it's really squandering energy that could be used more productively in my present relationships as a father, husband, worker and friend.

My friend suggested that if I was ready to forgive and let go, I could reclaim that trapped energy. He suggested I close my eyes and breathe deeply, recall the pain of the memory, ask for God's help and mercy, and then simply let go (perhaps by unclenching my fist or raising my palms to heaven). It worked—sort of. I did feel a little better, and so I will continue to practice this exercise with this particular memory until I have truly, completely and irrevocably let it go.

> **Now the Lord is the Spirit, and where the Spirit of the Lord is, there is freedom.**
>
> **2 Corinthians 3:17**

June 2   Secret intention

A friend of mine has a Saint Jude statue on the windowsill in his family's kitchen. (He's known best as the patron saint of "impossible causes.")

My friend's wife and kids know that if they have something special to pray for, whether it's a hopeless cause or not, they can write it down on a slip of paper and tuck it under the saint's statue. When others in the family see a slip of paper there, they know to add their own prayers for their family member's unspoken special intention.

It's as natural as breathing for them.

> *May mercy, peace, and love be yours in abundance.*

Jude 1:2

June 3   Living large

Neighbors a few blocks away are trying to supersize their life. They ripped the top off their nice-sized house and added two additional floors. They put a deck the size of Montana on the back of their house. They have a huge, big-screen TV you can see from three blocks away, and they drive an SUV the size of a mastodon.

As I pass their house on our nightly walk, I think of Saint Fiacre, the Irish priest who wound up in France trying to live a hermit's life. He was famed for his healing, and when he healed the child of a French nobleman he was granted "as much land as he could till in a day." Rather than hiring a team of horses and workers to maximize his holdings, he used only his staff and tilled a very small plot by himself, where he planted his healing herbs. It was all that he needed.

I wonder who is/was happier—my neighbors or Saint Fiacre?

> *Do not wear yourself out to get rich. Be wise enough to desist.*

Proverbs 23:5

June 4 — Sacred object

Hanging on the kitchen wall next to the phone is our family calendar. Lately I've come to see it as a sacred object. Our calendar comes from a religious organization, and so it lists holy days, fast days and feast days, as well as national holidays. I like how the church year and our family year blend together, but that's not why it's a sacred object.

I see how our life spills out of those little squares full of appointments, significant dates, holidays and reminders. Sprinkled throughout the year are celebrations, anniversaries, vacations and graduations that none of us wants to forget.

As I look at all the scribbling-in and scratching-out of appointments and commitments, I realize how our life is a constant ebb and flow, a changing of direction and then a turning back to where we began.

How we spend our days is a total gift to God. The sacred and the ordinary flow together in life. In fact, every day is sacred—even if we don't note it on the calendar.

> *How very good and pleasant it is when kindred*
> *live together in unity.*
>
> **Psalm 133:1**

June 5 — Trickle down theory

You've probably seen a cartoon that shows in a series of panels a boss yelling at a man, the man then yelling at his wife, the wife screaming at the older daughter, the older daughter picking on her younger brother, the brother tormenting his little sister, and the little sister kicking the dog.

Anyone in a family knows how quickly anger (or anxiety or fear) can sweep through the household, affecting everyone. How do you stop the cycle? Here are three suggested steps:

Observe your feelings rather than reacting to them. If you can acknowledge, without harsh judgment, that you are hurt or angry, you have at least half a chance of short-circuiting the spread of pain.

Ask God for help. When you turn the pain over to the care of the God who loves you, you'll be amazed how the external situation needn't change for your emotions to really turn around.

Do the "next right thing" in front of you. When you respond in love, you let go of pain and open your heart to the good things family life offers.

A soft answer turns away wrath.

Proverbs 15:1

June 6   Be not afraid

There are mornings when I awaken gripped by fear. I think of the many biblical passages where Jesus says, "Be not afraid," but I sit in my fear and I wonder, "How do you do that? How do you stop the fear?"

My one clue is that I have never stopped fear by thinking about it. Fear is a hungry monster that feeds on my attention. And so I try to look elsewhere and pour myself into the life that has been given to me.

I know there are towels in the dryer, and so I pull them out, fold them, and put them away. I set the table for my children's breakfast. I look up an address of a relative who's having a birthday and make a note to stop at the greeting card shop on the way to work. Suddenly, like fog in the morning sun, the fear thins and begins to evaporate.

God is with you in all that you do.

Genesis 21:22

114

June 7   Be not a "fixer"

Because we parents feel such responsibility for the welfare of our children, it's tempting for us to think we ought to fix, manage or control our kids' lives. And yet we know it's impossible to fix, manage or control any other human being. (Anyone who's tried to do so to a belligerent two-year-old or a cynical fifteen-year-old knows exactly what I'm saying.)

What we parents can do is *influence* our children toward good. Webster's defines *influence* as "the capacity or power of persons or things to be a compelling force on or produce effects on the actions, behavior, opinions, etc., of others."

The best way to do this is to offer love rather than commands, although some people have a hard time seeing the difference between the two. Spend some time today noticing when you use your influence with your children well and when you try to be a "fixer."

> *Trust in the Lord and do good; so you will live*
> *in the land and enjoy security.*
>
> **Psalm 37:3**

June 8   Back to the garden

My wife and I spent some time working in the garden this weekend. The kids helped. The neighbors were out in their yards. There was time for chatting and for quiet, contemplative work in nature.

We live in the middle of the city, yet our garden connects us to the wild. Birds chirp, rabbits hop by, butterflies meander, and bees hum from blossom to blossom. I even saw a humming bird skittering around.

Saturday morning we had all been mopey and dull. Looking ahead, the garden work seemed like a series of miserable chores.

But our moods changed within minutes of being out in the fresh air and sun. In mid afternoon, I suddenly realized that the closer I get to the earth the less distance I feel from myself and from my family. I have come to realize how artificial "real life" can be. No wonder you find so many shrines in gardens.

> *Ask the animals and they will teach you; the birds of the air, and they will tell you. Ask the plants of the earth and they will teach you.*
>
> **Job 12:7-8**

June 9 Empty promises, wild claims

The Bishop asked, "Do you reject Satan and all his empty promises?"

We were at a Catholic high school graduation and the graduates were invited to renew their baptismal vows. I don't know if the question struck the graduates, but it got me thinking. As a parent I couldn't help but hope that these young people, my daughter among them, had gained the ability to recognize empty promises and developed the character to reject them, no matter how alluring they might appear.

Satan's empty promises come to us as slogans that offer easy answers; God provides mysteries you have to enter into. Satan is all surface; God is all depth.

So try this: When your kids experience a disappointment stop and talk with them about their feelings. Often times the disappointment comes when an empty promise (for example, "Buy this type of clothing and you'll be popular") fails to pan out. Help them to spot the empty promise that led to their disappointment, but don't push it. It's a lifelong lesson, and there will be plenty of empty promises along the way.

*Beware of false prophets who come to you in
sheep's clothing, but inwardly are ravenous
wolves.*

Matthew 7:15

June 10   The present moment

There's a legend about Francis of Assisi that I think has a
message for parents. The beloved saint was working in his
garden one day, weeding rows of tomatoes and beans. It
was tedious work. A traveler came down the road, spotted Saint
Francis, and asked, "What would you be doing now if you knew
that today was the last day of your earthly life?"

Francis replied, "I would continue weeding this patch of garden." And that's just what he did.

The spiritual principle for parents illustrated by this story can be
summed up, "Be where you are, and do what you're doing." This
is so simple as to be easily missed or lost amid the distractions of
life. Think about it. How often are you in one place but your mind
and heart are occupied elsewhere? It happens to me all too frequently. For example, all day long I'll miss my kids, but when I'm
finally with them my mind is worrying about some deadline back
at work.

The challenge is to indeed be in the present moment with the
people we are with: making dinner, listening to a child's account of
the day, helping with homework, or simply taking a moment to
enjoy the flowers blooming in the backyard. The number one complaint among parents is that there's not enough time. And yet, we
have all the time there is: the present moment, which is the only one
that really exists.

*Blessed are the pure in heart, for they will see
God.*

Matthew 5:8

117

June 11   Take the initiative, Dad

My friend, Jim, volunteered to help on a project spon-
sored by The Fatherhood Initiative by reading hun-
dreds of essays written by kids about their dads. Reading between the lines, he discovered a lot of kids trying to understand what made their dads tick but completely baffled how to do
it.

Jim said, "After reading those essays I wanted to race home and
make some immediate changes in how I relate to my own kids. I
came to realize how much my mere presence means to them and
how much they wanted to know who their father really is."

During this season of Father's Day, realize the present your children are really looking for from you is your real presence in their
lives.

> *The king covered his face, and the king cried*
> *with a loud voice, "O my son Absalom, O Absa-*
> *lom, my son, my son!"*
>
> **2 Samuel 19:4**

June 12   Inside out

A friend of mine frequently offers this advice: Don't judge
your insides by everybody else's outsides. For years he felt
inadequate because he was so keenly aware of his insecu-
rities and feelings of incompetence. He knew how far short of his
own standards he regularly fell, and he often felt confused and be-
fuddled while those around him appeared confident, accomplished
and put together.

Over time he came to realize two things. First, most people feel
similar feelings of insecurity and inadequacy. Second, comparing
himself to others is a fool's game.

"Judge not," warns Jesus, who knows that comparisons are deadly. They not only distance us from others but shut us off from the flow of God's love. Comparing closes us up; it's borne of fear that God's love is limited and conditional.

Don't judge your insides by anybody else's outsides. Instead, love yourself, love your kids, and love the people you meet for who they are—mixed up insides and all.

Do not judge so that you may not be judged.

Matthew 7:1-2

June 13 — It's your job

I came across an interview with family expert Kathleen Chesto that appeared in *U.S. Catholic.* The opening paragraph grabbed me. The interviewers asked, "What should religious educators be telling parents?"

Chesto replied: "I really believe we, as a church, have to tell parents that we can't give faith to their children. As long as we tell them we can do it, they'll let us. We're all busy. If you tell me you'll wash my car every week, I'll let you. So we have to come right out and say the church is going to help you, but it cannot do the work for you. You have to learn to depend on your own faith."

Summer is starting and formal religious education programs may be waning, but this season offers many opportunities for you to feed your kids' faith—including time for stories, for closeness, for nature, for visiting older relatives, and for sharing a little bit of what you believe and why. Make a point this week of sharing at least one bit of spiritual wisdom with each of your children.

As for me and my household, we will serve the Lord.

Joshua 24:15

June 14   Life lessons

S ome of my most effective faith lessons were learned watching my parents. Maybe that's true for you too. Dad went to Mass most mornings, and when I became an altar boy I enjoyed getting up early and spending that time with him. Even more impressive to me, though, was realizing how my dad truly sees the image and likeness of God in everyone he meets.

Mom teaches in a special religious education program and has for twenty years. Before that she helped at the school library. Before that she regularly gathered with a bunch of women to make bandages for cancer patients. And before that she participated in a string of other volunteer efforts in the parish.

My parents wouldn't think that any of this was worth commenting on. It's just what believers do, they'd say. It's how you order your life.

Be doers of the word and not merely hearers.

James 1:22

June 15   Litanies

W hen our children were young they'd pray at night: "God bless Mommy and Daddy, God bless Grandma Marge and Grandpa Pat, God bless Grammy Pearl and Grandpa Jim in heaven, God bless Uncle Pat...."

I'm glad they knew they had a host of people they could pray for and who would be praying for them. The cadence of their prayer reminded me of the litanies we would recite when I was a kid: "Saint Laurence, pray for us. Saint Lucy, pray for us. Saints Felicity and Perpetua, pray for us...." Such exotic names, names of people from distant lands and distant times, all ready to pray for me!

Being a kid who often got in trouble, I welcomed all the help I could get. I still do. I hope my kids do too.

Lift up your prayer for the remnant that is left.

2 Kings 19:4

June 16 — What to pray for?

Her daughter was worried about a problem with her friends from school. Talking about it further wasn't going to help. Mom asked, "Have you prayed about it?"

Her daughter answered, "Yeah, and that's why I'm so angry. I asked God to make this better and I still have the problem." She folded her arms across her chest and pouted. "I don't think God wants me to be happy."

Mom replied, "I truly believe that God wants you to be happy. It's just that God might have a different idea of what will make you happy. Try praying to see what lesson God has for you in this."

Her daughter made no answer, but you could see the wheels spinning, her mind expanding to make room for this new idea.

*When you are praying, do not heap up empty
phrases as the Gentiles do; for they think that
they will be heard because of their many words.
For your Father knows what you need before
you ask him.*

Matthew 6:6-8

June 17 — Two dads

There were two dads at the party accompanied by a three-year-old daughter. They both were paying close attention to their child. One was full of concern at how his daugh-

121

ter's behavior was affecting others. He was worried how what she did or didn't do would be received and how it would reflect back on him. His anxiety made her anxious and rebellious and confused.

The other dad paid attention because he cared about how his daughter was faring at the party. He wasn't spoiling her; he was being mindful of her and making sure she had what she needed to be a sweet child enjoying a party. His underlying concern for her soothed his daughter and she was calm, happy and sure of herself.

Both dads were me, and was my poor daughter ever confused!

You reap whatever you sow.

Galatians 6:7

June 18 — Watch your "but," part 1

Amen's group I belong to has helped me realize how often I use the word "but" when "and" would be more accurate. For example, I can say, "I love my daughter, but I'm angry with her." Or, "I am a kind and loving parent, but I am often selfish and petty." The "but" seems to negate or diminish the first part of the sentence. It can make both sentiments feel mutually exclusive.

When I try the same sentence using "and" instead of "but," I often discover a new insight. I can love my daughter *and* be mad at her. I can be a kind and loving parent *and* also be selfish and petty at times. It's important to give both sides of reality their due in our parental minds and hearts.

Language is powerful. Pay attention to when you're sticking your "but" where it doesn't belong.

Teach me your way, O Lord, that I may walk in your truth.

Psalm 86:11

June 19   Watch your "but," part 2

My friend, Kevin, warns me: "Don't be a 'sorry but.'" He describes this as someone who always says something like, "I'm sorry that I talked to you that way, but you drive me crazy at times."

"It's amazing to me how much more powerful apologies become when I leave out the explanations and excuses," Kevin concludes.

Another friend, Greg, agrees. "I try to teach my kids (and remind myself) that the only acceptable apology consists of four parts: 1) I was wrong; 2) I'm sorry; 3) I accept the consequences of my action; 4) I will try not to do it again. If any of these four elements are followed by a 'but,' then we have to start all over again until we get it right—without any 'buts.'"

> *If another sins, and if there is repentance, you must forgive.*

Luke 17:3

June 20   Apprentice

I worked a few summers years ago helping out on a landscape crew. The crew chief, Bill Cork, was a true artist. He would go into an overgrown thicket with a pruning saw and hand shears, and a few hours later you would swear the scene had been designed and carefully planted and nurtured for years. He could look at a tree that was twisted and overgrown and see within a tangled mess its elegant beauty. He reminded me of Michelangelo's line about his sculpture of David: "I carved away everything that was not David."

Bill taught all of us on his crew how to see. Even now when I'm driving down a country road I'll look at a tree, searching for its elegant underlying structure.

Raising kids with faith is much like the apprenticeship I had with Bill. Through our teaching, but mostly through the way we ourselves see, parents offer kids eyes to see. Let's hope we teach our kids how to see the beautiful grand design of God in all things.

> *The Lord does not see as mortals; they look on the outward appearance, but the Lord looks on the heart.*

1 Samuel 16:7

June 21   Awesome!

The piped-in music in the maternity ward was playing Stevie Wonder's song "Isn't She Lovely?" within minutes after my first child was born. I couldn't have made a better selection on my own. I was so full of emotion I literally wanted to shout from the roof of the hospital that the world ought to stop and pay attention to the miracle that had just occurred.

Parenting begins in awe. From our very flesh and blood new life is created. And what is created is not just mere flesh and blood but a new and unique person with the spark of soul within. That morning my identity changed. From that day forward I would always be somebody's Daddy. And from that day forward, I would know what miracles look like.

> *When a woman is in labor she has pain, because her hour has come. But when her child is born, she no longer remembers the anguish because of the joy of having brought a human being into the world.*

John 16:21

June 22   Free gift, part 4

Have you hung in there when you wanted to throw in the towel? That's Fortitude. One more free gift of the Holy Spirit.

Be strong in the grace that is in Christ Jesus; and what you have heard from me through many witnesses entrust to faithful people who will be able to teach others well.

2 Timothy 2:2

June 23   It's a promise

When each of my daughters was still quite young, I'd find a moment alone with her to tell her this: "I want you to promise me that when you get to be a teenager and don't want to tell me anything anymore you will still sit and talk to me."

And they would look at me quizzically and figure this was one of those crazy adult requests that kids aren't supposed to understand. I never expected them to. I just wanted them to remember. This little speech wasn't for their benefit; it was for mine. It was a wild and hopeful prayer.

Incidentally, it's a prayer that came true.

I cry to you and you do not answer me; I stand, and you merely look at me.

Job 30:20

125

June 24   Green Giant

I'm all for having younger kids memorize elements of their faith as presented by the church. It's a great way to populate their minds with truths that start out as pat answers but over time blossom into mysteries.

But it's important to get these catechetical gems right. When I was a kid, for example, we all learned the answer to the question, "Who is God?" I can still snap back that answer, "God is the supreme being who created all things." One kid in my first grade class, however, misunderstood Sister Vincent, and for days he was reciting, "God is the string bean who created all things."

I wonder if he became a vegetarian.

> *So then, brothers and sisters, stand firm and*
> *hold fast to the traditions that you were taught,*
> *either by word of mouth or by our letter.*
>
> **2 Thessalonians 2:15**

June 25   Hold on!

One golden summer my kids and I spent a week along the beautiful shoreline of Lake Michigan. We stayed with lots of family members in a big house just steps from the shore. One afternoon we went down to the beach after the girls had their nap and the waves were high. I was still setting up our spot on the beach, and the girls were eager to get into the water, so Aunt Marie and Uncle Johnny grabbed hold of their hands and walked them out into the turbulent lake. There, holding hands, they all withstood wave after wave crashing into them. Clinging to their great aunt and uncle, the girls were perfectly safe.

Years later at another family gathering, Aunt Marie and Uncle Johnny slowly make their way up our walkway. My daughters rush out to greet them, and this time it's the oldsters who are grabbing on to the youngsters for safety as they all climb our front steps.

This, to me, is the circle of life.

> *Maintain constant love for one another, for love covers a multitude of sins. Be hospitable to one another without complaining.*
>
> **1 Peter 4: 8-9**

June 26   You move too fast

My daughter came home from babysitting one night repeating some of the cute phrases her charges had said. "When we're coloring or cutting things out," she said, "the boys will recite to themselves, 'Slow and steady, steady and slow. That's the way we always go!'" It's a good mantra.

"The soul likes to go slow," advises a spiritually adept friend. And while I have known my soul to enjoy speedboats and downhill skiing, what I know of my life is that my soul gets way too little time to go slow. As summer unfolds and days are long, I have the chance to slow my pace and the pace of my family. So slow me down, Lord, and let me be a good example to my family.

> *Those who wait for the Lord shall renew their strength. They shall mount up with wings like eagles. They shall run and not be weary.*
>
> **Isaiah 40:31**

June 27   Try easier

I think a lot of what keeps people, especially busy people in families, from making spiritual progress is that they think they're going to have to add yet another burden onto their already filled shoulders. Yet I've often found when I've sought spiritual advice that I'm encouraged to try "easier," not "harder."

Sometimes the best thing we can do for ourselves spiritually is to take a moment in a busy day to simply be mindful and breathe. If you cannot find this kind of down time, then you might have to figure out why your life is no longer your own. And if it is not yours, whose is it?

P.S. To those with infants, ignore this meditation for now and revisit it in six months—after you've had a full night's sleep.

The spirit indeed is willing, but the flesh is weak.

Mark 14:38

June 28   When kids know best

One summer, years ago, we noticed our daughter, Judy, was no longer hanging out with a friend whom we especially liked. We kept asking, "Have you heard from Lulu?" and nudging her to call her friend. Judy evaded our questions and ignored our promptings, even when we pressed.

Years later we heard the rest of the story. That summer the girl, we'll call her "Lulu," was having a rough time. She was experimenting with drugs and hanging out with kids we wouldn't have wanted our daughter to be with. Judy had enough sense to let the friendship go dormant for a while, and she had enough character to protect her friend's privacy. Lulu made it through that rough patch, and the friendship continued later.

Sometimes it pays to trust your kids.

The wise mind will know the time and the way.

Ecclesiastes 8:5

June 29   What I did for love

My older daughter, Judy, spent her junior year of college studying in Ecuador. I was fortunate to be able to visit her there. In addition to my own luggage, I took a huge suitcase of supplies that my wife had packed for Judy. When I got to the customs station in Ecuador—a room with a huge wall of windows where those waiting for arrivals gathered to watch for their loved ones—the customs agent opened the bag my wife had packed. He reached in and pulled out a pair of dainty panties and, without cracking a smile, asked, "Anything to declare?"

At times like that it pays to remember, "This will make a good story at future family gatherings."

> *I know your works, your toil, and your patient endurance.*

Revelations 2:2

June 30   Jesus' family values

Jesus was pretty much against the idea of clannishness, where people cared about only those in their own extended family. He tried to break down the barriers of nation, race, group, clan and family.

So does that mean families don't matter or that Jesus didn't think they were important? On the contrary. Where else are people going to learn the lessons Jesus taught about service and respect and inclusiveness, if not in their families?

Too often kids come to school already believing that one ethnic group (their own) is better than another. They learn this in their families. But they can unlearn that lesson there too. They can learn the new truth that Jesus taught: that we are to love one another (meaning everyone) as we love ourselves.

Families shouldn't build walls to keep the world out, but we should build bridges out to the world.

> *So we, who are many, are one body in Christ, and individually we are members of one another.*

Romans 12:5

July 1   What year is this?

We continue to be influenced by all our yesterdays. Some-times that delayed influence gets in the way of our being the kind of parent we want to be.

I read an example of this in *Redbook* magazine's "Be a Better Parent" feature. The article was on being more intentional when we say "yes" or "no" to our kids. One child therapist reported, "I was working with a mother with three sons. The first boy asked if he could go outside and play, and the mother said yes immediately. The second son asked the same thing, and the mother snapped at him. I asked her, 'Whom does that second child remind you of?' She admitted he reminds her of her brother, with whom she always had a difficult relationship. Once she saw that, she was able to treat that son much more fairly and rationally."

Self-knowledge is one of the most powerful tools to becoming a better parent. Be a caring observer of your own behavior, and you'll see clues to how old issues and wounds creep into today's relationships. Cleaning away such old business can make for an easier rest of the summer for you and your family.

> *The kingdom of heaven may be compared to a*
> *king who gave a wedding banquet for his son.*
> **Matthew 22: 2**

July 2   Slowly and well

In the past couple of days I've heard it three times. I ask, "How's your summer going?" and I hear, "Way too fast!"

Is there a way to slow your summer down? Probably not to the leisurely speed we experienced it as ten-year-olds. (Although with all the sports and camps and classes kids have during the summer these days, maybe they think summer is going by "way too fast" as well.)

A lesson I learned from my wife is to take a twenty-minute "quiet time" early each morning during the summer. The sun rises earlier, so why not get up a little earlier and spend that time letting your soul catch up with your busy life?

As parents we're always in demand. In terms of balance we probably tilt heavier toward providing service for others than tending to our own inner self. But if we begin our day giving time to our soul, we'll undoubtedly find that life seems to proceed at a more manageable and enjoyable pace. We'll have more patience and joy to share with our children throughout the day.

> *As long as I am in the world I am the light of the world.*
>
> **John 9:5**

July 3   A taste of freedom

There are a million people along the lakefront and we're all getting along. Black and white and brown and every other shade of human being are here—sitting on blankets, listening to the orchestra, waiting for the fireworks to begin.

Cops are wisecracking with bikers; strangers strike up conversations in the long lines waiting at the port-a-potties, people whose relatives are fighting in other countries are sharing wine with people who oppose the war. We all make room for one another as every inch of lawn space gets put to good use.

During the fireworks, our eyes are all turned upward and we join in collective "oohs" and "ahhs." I don't normally enjoy crowds, and part of me wishes I were watching this on TV at home. But I realize that this annual celebration is about our freedom to be different from one another yet part of the same country. This is a lesson I am glad my kids are here to see.

> *I will plant them upon their land, and they shall*
> *never again be plucked up out of the land that I*
> *have given them, says the Lord.*

Amos 9:15

July 4   Independence from fear

I came across one of my old journals yesterday, and it contained a lesson for me about freedom. I noticed that many of the journal entries were taken up with worries about situations I can scarcely remember or that turned out fine—and would have turned out fine even without all that worry.

At the time I wrote about them, though, those fears dominated many pages and therefore many minutes, hours and days of my life. Especially when it comes to my family, it seems, fear is my copilot.

As you celebrate Independence Day, why not ask God to free you from needless fear? I intend to.

> *Thus says the Lord, the God of Israel: Let my*
> *people go!*

Exodus 5:1

July 5   Teeter-totter, bread and water

At the neighborhood playground, I observe two children on the teeter-totter. An age-old ritual is taking place. The bigger, heavier kid is "tottered" down low while the other kid is "teetering" high above the ground.

"What will you give me if I let you down?" asks the bigger kid.

Then, without warning, he lets his side shoot up while the smaller kid slams down with a bang.

"Hey! Why'd you do that?" the little one cries.

I stop to think. This is not unlike what I do to my kids when I'm too busy for them. I abruptly and hurtfully drop them from my care. I know it hurts them, but unlike the kid on the playground I'm deeply sorry about it.

> *Because the Lord your God is a merciful God,*
> *he will neither abandon you nor destroy you; he*
> *will not forget the covenant with your ancestors*
> *that he swore to them.*

Deuteronomy 4:31

July 6 Because

Because I've caught crayfish in a creek by the railroad tracks....

Because I've lolled in a hammock after lunch, reading Aquaman comic books while waiting a full hour before returning to the pool at the YMCA....

Because I've chased grasshoppers by day and fireflies by night, watched a zillion stars light up a blackened sky, and tasted the sweetness of a root beer float on a country highway after dark....

Because I've heard scary stories told, and told a few as well, and walked a wooded path with friends I knew were pals for keeps, built a club house, played "red rover," swung on a rope to splash in a slow brown river, rolled down dunes and watched a turtle doze in dappled sunlight....

Because I have done these things, my heart knows why Jesus said you must be like a child before you enter the kingdom of heaven.

> *A child who gathers in summer is prudent.*

Proverbs 10:5

July 7   One percent will do!

At one time or another, all parents feel overwhelmed. Maybe your child is facing illness, or out of nowhere his or her grades are dropping for no apparent reason. Maybe family life seems to have become a battleground, or a child you were formerly close to hardly acknowledges that you exist.

Whenever I begin to feel that a particular parenting challenge is way too much for me, I think of a friend of mine who has a Post-It Note next to his computer reading, "Do your one percent!" I asked him what that was all about.

He answered that he'd once heard a sermon that said we only need to provide one percent of the solution to any problem—God will provide the other ninety-nine percent.

The corollary, of course, is that if we don't do our one percent, we're blocking God's ninety-nine percent from taking effect in our lives.

> **The Lord answer you in the day of trouble.**
>
> **Psalm 20:1**

July 8   You must remember this

A Norwegian legend says that before we're born God plants a kiss upon our soul. Throughout our lives, our soul remembers that kiss and longs to return to God.

There is no doubt something inside each of us longs for God. It's good to acknowledge that longing when we're with our children, for their souls were also kissed by God.

> **As a deer longs for flowing streams, so my soul longs for you, O God.**
>
> **Psalm 42:1**

July 9 — Spirit dead

I had a friend when I was growing up with whom I'd often get into trouble. He was always full of ideas that seemed good at the time.

I was glad that my parents didn't label him a "bad kid." They saw his exuberance for what it was: a good and lively spirit, no matter how misguided. They recognized that despite his propensity for trouble he was deeply spiritual. The opposite of being spiritual is not being naughty. It's being apathetic. It's having no life, no juice, no joy.

It's good for me to remember my old friend when the spirit in my kids is driving me nuts!

> *I will pour out my spirit on all your flesh; your sons and your daughters shall prophesy, your old men shall dream dreams.*
>
> **Joel 2:28**

July 10 — The baby did it!

How's the new grandson?" I asked my pal.

"He's great. But his older brother has already realized how convenient it is to have someone else to blame."

"Really? What happened?"

"I asked the older boy if he'd made a mess. He looked down sheepishly and said, 'Maybe the baby did it.'"

The impulse to blame someone else goes all the way back to Adam ("The woman made me do it") and Eve ("The devil made me do it") and echoes through the generations. We do our children a great service when we help them learn to take responsibility for their actions.

I have one suggestion though: When your children finally do

own up to a misdeed don't greet their admissions with punishment and shame. As William Damon, author of *The Moral Child* writes, "There is no more effective facilitator of moral development than fostering children's willingness to take responsibility for good and bad deeds."

> *David said to Nathan, "I have sinned against the Lord." Nathan said to David, "Now the Lord has put away your sin; you shall not die.*
>
> 1 Samuel 12:13

July 11   We're banking on you

I've found a lot of wisdom in Steven Covey's *The Seven Habits of Highly Effective Families*. One potent and practical suggestion he proposes is the concept of the Emotional Bank Account. The idea is that our relationship with others can be seen as an Emotional Bank Account, and the balance of trust and good will we've built up in the account determines how well we can communicate and get along with the other person. "Full" accounts make for smooth sailing; "overdrawn" accounts will be rocky and quarrelsome.

Doing thoughtful, unsolicited favors, respecting a child's request for privacy, keeping your commitments all count as deposits. Nagging, belittling and neglecting are examples of withdrawals. Any action that builds trust in the relationship builds up your account; those that tear down a child's self-esteem drain it. Some days it's chilling to think through a day and adjust your balance!

Just a note of caution—deposits need to be sincerely made with no strings attached. If they're manipulative and you're expecting an immediate return on your investment, you're in the wrong market.

Then the one who had received the five talents came forward, bringing five more talents, saying, "Master, you handed over to me five talents; see, I have made five more talents.'

Matthew 25:20

July 12   Abundance

The way kids squabble over toys, treats and television you'd think we lived in a land of scarcity rather than the richest society in the history of the world. Children aren't alone at this. I see such behavior in the workplace as well. We're all prone to acting like starving people fighting over the last crust of bread.

Recently at church I heard the story of the loaves and fishes. In this story, Jesus countered a prevailing notion—then and now—that what we most need in life is in short supply. By gathering people into manageable circles, blessing the food that was readily available, and teaching people to share, he revealed that what we truly need is available in abundance.

When we parents fall into the scarcity mode our children do the same. When we all feel confident in God's abundance we discover that we already have all we need.

And taking the five loaves and the two fish, he looked up to heaven, and blessed and broke them, and gave them to the disciples to set before the crowd. And all ate and were filled.

Luke 9:14-17

Not as the world gives

After his resurrection, Jesus greeted people with "Peace I leave with you, my peace I give to you."

Yet Jesus had a concept of peace different from the indulgent tranquility portrayed in the ads for Caribbean beach vacations, luxury cars or soothing herbal tea. Jesus was talking about a deeper peace altogether. What kind of peace did Jesus have in mind? This is how it might look for families:

- the peace that comes from doing the right thing for our kids rather than taking the easy way out;
- the peace of living up to our own values and standards about curfew, clothes and media choices, even though our kids may complain loud and long;
- the peace of knowing that God is acting in the life of our family, using even our foibles for good;
- the peace of understanding that if we are open and willing as parents, God will work wonders with our children.

> *Peace I leave with you; my peace I give to you. I do not give to you as the world gives.*
>
> **John 14:27**

July 14 Come one, come all

My family and I recently went to celebrate the twenty-fifth anniversary of a friend's ordination. He's pastor of one of Chicago's poorest Catholic parishes, home to many of America's most recent immigrants. In the parish school literally dozens of languages are spoken.

During the celebration representatives of numerous groups came up to say a few words. They said how grateful they were that Father Simon had welcomed them and made them feel at home.

The Mass was beautiful and involved touching elements from each culture represented in the parish. The choir sang in Spanish, Vietnamese and Tagalog. Prayers were voiced in many other languages. What united us all was our focus on God as the Parent of us all. Through our simple acts of worship, we came to realize we are brothers and sisters to each other. I'm glad my kids were there to see this truth so vividly revealed.

You shall love your neighbor as yourself.

Leviticus 19:18

July 15   Free gift, part 5

Are you open-minded? Do you let go of superstitions, prejudices and intellectual pettiness? That's the gift of Knowledge, a further gift of the Holy Spirit.

The wise lay up knowledge, but the babbling of a fool brings ruin near.

Proverbs 10:14

July 16   A dose of silliness

I remember when my daughters were about four and six and I was in a foul mood. I actually chided them by barking, "Don't be silly!" They stopped what they were doing, looked at me like I had three heads, and asked in all seriousness, "Why not?"

I had no good answer for them. What I had instead was a realization that I could use a good dose of silliness myself. So I stopped doing whatever it was I was trying to do (probably put all the toys in order yet again) and joined in their make-believe games. What a blessing that turned out to be.

Thankfully, on that day (and many others) I had my kids to show me the way. This week look for wisdom from your children and from those friends who have maintained their childlike qualities. The kid inside you will be delighted!

> *Then shall the young women rejoice in the dance, and the young men and the old shall be merry. I will turn their mourning into joy, I will comfort them, and give them gladness for sorrow.*
>
> **Jeremiah 31:13**

July 17   Buon apetito!

S ince my return from a family vacation to Italy, people have asked me to name my favorite part of the trip. I think of the great views, the amazing art, the quaint cobblestone streets, the grand churches, and Venice's enchanting canals, but then I settle on my clear favorite—the meals.

Now I'm perhaps the world's least adventurous eater (except when it comes to dessert) and so the prospect of testing the local cuisine wasn't the draw for me. One life lesson the Italians can surely teach me, however, is how to make the most out of meals. By the time I was ready to leave Italy it was easy for me to sit for hours over dinner, watching the passersby, sharing thoughts from the day, laughing and teasing gently, and simply being together with my family. That lesson—to realize how deeply powerful it is to share a meal together—is the one souvenir I really wanted to bring back from the trip. And so far, it's working.

It's not easy to get a young family settled around the table, I know. And some meals—perhaps most—are going to be hectic, messy affairs. But do what you can to slow things down, entice people to linger, engage in conversation. In our fast-food culture, the family meal is still the greatest antidote to the forces that attempt to pull us in a million directions.

By the way, what's for dessert?

> *When these days were completed, the king gave for all the people present in the citadel of Susa, both great and small, a banquet lasting for seven days, in the court of the garden of the king's palace.*

Esther 1:5

July 18 — Summertime blues

He hates to see his son look so blue. Normally, the boy smiles like sunshine. He bounds through life radiating energy and joy. But not today, nor for the past few days.

"What's wrong?" Dad asks.

"Nothin'," replies the son, looking glum and picking at his shoelace.

"Are you sure? Because if there's ever anything wrong…"

"Da-ad! I'm fine. Can't you just leave me alone?"

And deep inside, Dad thinks, "No, I can't leave you alone. I can't bear to see you this way. I want to pick you up like when you were a toddler and fell down and skinned your knee. I want to kiss the boo-boo and make the pain go away. It kills me to be unable to do that for you anymore."

But he knows that those emotions are all about himself and not at all helpful to the boy in front of him. And he says instead, "Sure, son. Okay. But if you need anything…"

> *For there is still a vision for the appointed time…. If it seems to tarry, wait for it, it will not delay.*
>
> **Habakkuk 2:3**

July 19   Don't lose touch

W hen my daughters started to become young women my signs of affection toward them became more stilted and tentative. A friend of mine pulled me aside and gave me a warning. She said it still hurts her to remember how her father pulled away from her as she grew older and she never felt his hug again. "Every daughter needs her father's hug," she said, "and I suspect that every son does too." And so I began to hug my girls again, because every child needs hugs.

And we parents do too.

> *Beloved, since God loved us so much, we also ought to love one another.*
>
> **1 John 4:11**

July 20   Heaven

T he survey asked people what they thought heaven would be like. Some described palaces and thrones. Others talked of unending feasts and festivals. For me, heaven is plopping myself in an inner tube on Ackley Lake and floating lazily in the sun with my family as time stands still.

Light is sweet, and it is pleasant for the eyes to see the sun.

Ecclesiastes 11:7

July 21   "Ain't nobody happy"

Am I the only one who can change a toilet paper roll around here?" When I heard myself voicing this complaint loudly I realized it was time to find an attitude adjustment.

Life's little upsets don't usually bother me, so when I start picking on everyone around me over toilet paper I know it's time to take care of myself a little.

As parents we spend much of our lives taking care of others. That's just a fact. But that doesn't mean we can't also make sure our own need for rest, respect, care and fun get their due.

I once saw an apron a friend was wearing that said: "If Momma ain't happy, ain't nobody happy!"

Same goes for Daddy.

> *Six days you shall work, but on the seventh day you shall rest; even in plowing time and in harvest time you shall rest.*

Exodus 34:21

July 22   Praise God!

Praise God:
- for sun shining through water sprinklers;
- for blue skies the color they were when we were kids;
- for long, slow days when there seems to be time enough for every task;

- for leisurely talks over backyard fences;
- for the sound of children playing games;
- for cats sleeping in sunny windowsills;
- for dogs who lope and leap and snag a Frisbee in midair;
- for the tinkling of bells that signal the ice cream man is on his way.

For summer, praise God.

> *O Lord, how manifold are your works! In wisdom you have made them all, the earth is full of your creatures.*
>
> **Psalm 104:24**

July 23   The unimaginable

The tearful parents on the news cannot hide their agony. Their child has been kidnapped, surely a parent's worst nightmare. The whole town and neighboring communities have been mobilized, and thousands of people respond. They feel drawn to do whatever they can possibly do.

As I get ready for bed my prayers are with that family. Before I'm able to drift off to sleep I must get up one more time to check that the doors are locked and the windows are latched. There are just some things a parent should never have to endure.

> *Lead me to the rock that is higher than I, for you are my refuge.*
>
> **Psalm 61:2-3**

I recently heard a martial arts expert say, "It's important to keep your friends close, but it's more important to keep your enemies even closer." As it turns out, he wasn't talking only about human enemies, but especially the "enemies within" that can so easily trip us up.

This advice reminded me of a practice I was encouraged to do as I was growing up—a nightly examination of conscience. This was a review of the day and my activities so I could become more aware of the good, the bad and the ugly of what I had done and what I had failed to do.

Unfortunately, the way I took this advice amplified my self-criticism and distrust of my own good qualities. I went about it as though I were on a witch-hunt. It doesn't have to be that way. Instead of being punitive, this practice can simply help us become more awake to the traits and behaviors and emotions we have that we would prefer to keep in the shadows. We can bring them into the light where they are less likely to ambush us.

I try to encourage this habit of self-awareness in my daughters. If they know themselves, they can be aware of their true goodness. If they can be curious and compassionate observers of themselves, they can gain confidence that everything they uncover can be redeemed—even their worst enemies within.

> *Who can hide in secret places so that I cannot see them? Do I not fill heaven and earth? says the Lord.*
>
> **Jeremiah 23:24**

July 25   Visit to the zoo, part 1

Y ou were less than two and I took you to the zoo. I wanted to show you the bears and the giraffes, the zebras and
the gorillas. I was thrilled to see that they were training an
elephant, walking her right down a pathway less than five feet
away from us. "Look, look at the big elephant!" I urged.

But you, a queen in her stroller, were unfazed by this mass of
gray wrinkles and flapping ears. You were too busy leaning forward, following the antics of a chipmunk frolicking free in the un-
derbrush.

From then on I knew that the real treat at the zoo was watching
you.

> **God said, "Let the earth bring forth living crea-
> tures of every kind: cattle and creeping things
> and wild animals of the earth of every kind."**
>   **Genesis 1:24**

July 26   Visit to the zoo, part 2

N ow you're going on twenty. You've spent a year away at
college, and your return home is a challenge for us all.
You've changed. You've grown. You choose your own
hours. You report to no one. I look at you and wonder—are you
still the little girl I knew?

We make a date, just the two of us, to go to the zoo. We've both
been working hard—you with exams, me with too many deadlines.
The hot day finds us sluggish and perhaps not up to a joyful romp.
We end up in a new exhibit watching the otters. Their playfulness
attracts a crowd, and we get separated on either side of a large
group of moms and their kids. The moms decide it's time to go.

One little girl about four or five has been watching the otter dive and swim at eye level, inches away on the other side of the glass. She doesn't want to leave this scene of playfulness and joy. "Tiffany! We're leaving, and I mean *now*!" cries her mother from outside the exit door. Tiffany knows her mother means business and moves to go. But in a flash she turns quickly, and just as the otter reaches the point where they come eye-to-eye she plants a big smooch on the glass. Then she runs to catch up with her group.

Immediately, I search you out. Our eyes meet. I see your delight at the gift young Tiffany bestowed on all who had eyes to see. And I know in an instant that my daughter is home. We go off to sit in the shade and talk, finally, about how life has been for both of us this past year.

> *Do you have eyes, and fail to see? Do you have ears, and fail to hear? And do you not remember?*
>
> **Mark 8:18**

July 27   Discipline

Kids need lots of discipline—their parents' self-discipline, that is. What does parental self-discipline look like?

We need to be there when we say we will; follow through on our promises; not take our problems out on our kids; be consistent with our rules; be consistent with our praise.

Most of all, if we need help we need to get it...sooner rather than later.

> *Know therefore that the Lord your God is God, the faithful God who maintains covenant loyalty with those who love him and keep his commandments, to a thousand generations.*
>
> **Deuteronomy 7:9**

July 28   The new bike

The boy got a new bike for his birthday and was eager to try it, but he didn't want to use the training wheels. He wanted to ride the two-wheeler just like his brother and the other older kids.

And so up and down the sidewalk went father and son, with lots of shouts and spills and a growing desperation on both their parts.

"I know you can do this," said the dad, "if only you'll relax and let the bike do the work."

The man gives a big push and lets go, and the boy finally gets it. He feels the breeze on his face and the sheer glee of coasting along on a bike. He starts pedaling like a little madman and is on his way. Hooray!

The dad stands and watches. He utters a silent prayer. "God, I find it hard to let go and just enjoy the ride. Thanks for the extra pushes you provide, just when I need them."

> *For while we live, we are always being given up*
> *to death for Jesus' sake, so that the life of Jesus*
> *may be made visible in our mortal flesh.*
>
> **2 Corinthians 4:12**

July 29   Beginner's mind

Some neighbor kids are over while I'm working on a new out-door patio. A few of them want to help, so I begin to show one of them how to level the sand. He grabs the tool from my hand, and to every instruction I give he cuts in with, "I know. I know."

He bungles the job.

I'm like him at the job of parenting. I want to jump right into things without listening or accepting the wisdom others are more than ready to offer. A sufficient number of flops, however, has shown me the truth of what the Greek philosopher Epictetus said: "It is impossible to begin to learn that which one thinks one already knows."

> *Now the Lord came and stood there, calling as before, "Samuel! Samuel!" And Samuel said, "Speak, for your servant is listening."*
>
> 1 Samuel 3:10

July 30 "Fore" warned

I'm not the type of guy who believes that life is like a game of golf. Life is nowhere near as excruciating as golf—at least the way I play it. But I did learn a lesson recently that applies to my parenting. It has to do with making a lousy shot—something I'm quite expert at.

For years I've gotten mad at myself when I hooked a ball far off the fairway. Yet often when I get to my ball and line up the next shot, I'm surprised to find I'm not all that bad off. Sometimes, in fact, I've discovered a little-known short cut to the hole!

Likewise, if I'm dealing with a difficult situation with one of my kids I can build it up in my mind until it becomes a catastrophe. I get worried and angry and anxious. Yet if I just try to do "the next right thing" the situation usually doesn't end all that badly.

Mark Twain said, "I have known a lot of troubles in my life, most of which never happened."

> *I rejoice, because I have complete confidence in you.*
>
> 2 Corinthians 7:16

The mom handed out ten cups of Kool-Aid. The kids, thirsty and eager to return to their games, gulped the drinks down without a word—all except one young boy, who stood before her and said, "Thank you very much. That was very good."

She didn't even know this boy. He was somebody's friend from two blocks over. She thought, "I hope my kids see more of him." As she cleaned up the mess the mother had a smile on her face and a bit of hope in her heart.

Were not ten made clean? But the other nine, where are they? Was none of them found to return and give praise to God except this foreigner?

Luke 17:17

August 1   Eye-to-eye...and beyond

Here's a quick tip to better connect with your kids, your spouse, or anyone in your life with whom you want to be closer: When you're talking with them stop and look them in the left eye. That's right, the *left* eye.

A friend of mine who studies many mystical spiritual practices tells me that in certain traditions looking into another person's left eye is the way to connect with that person's soul. I find this practice helps me focus better and be more present to the person I'm talking to, allowing me to be more intentional about my desire to connect with those I love.

> *Your eye is the lamp of your body. If the eye is healthy, your whole body is full of light.*
>
> **Luke 11:34**

August 2   Treasure hunt

Jesus advised us to make for ourselves "money bags that do not wear out."

I wonder what such a wallet or purse would look like for parents—one that doesn't get depleted by tuition bills, charges for back-to-school clothes and supplies, or the endless stream of requests for lab fees, fund raisers and field trips. But I suspect Jesus had a more valuable kind of money bag in mind—one that purchases a new frame of mind.

Jesus was talking about keeping our eye on the true prize for our children—that they "love one another as I have loved you"—instead of on their immediate and temporary wishes. The good news is that such treasure is readily and abundantly available to all of us—no matter how bad our credit rating has been in the past.

Make purses for yourselves that do not wear out,
an unfailing treasure in heaven, where no thief
comes near and no moth destroys.

Luke 12:33

August 3   Sweet mercy

A s a seventh grade teacher, my wife Kathleen is continually running into questions of justice versus mercy. Since the emotional lives of thirteen-year-olds tend to be erratic to the extreme, and because Kathleen is accessible to them for such a good part of their day, she's often been hurt by something goofy her students will say or do.

Kathleen needs to hold them accountable yet still let them know forgiveness is not only possible but offered to all. She's very clear when they cross a line they shouldn't, and she makes them admit they were wrong and apologize, which is an important part of their overall education. But after a child has done what he or she is asked to do in the way of "penance," my wife makes a point of seeking out the child and saying, "As far as I'm concerned, the slate is clean."

And she never, ever brings the situation up again to throw it in the kid's face at a later date.

And if the same person sins against you seven
times a day, and turns back to you seven times
and says, "I repent," you must forgive.

Luke 17:4

August 4   Notice the closeness

Some parents may feel inadequate to the task of introducing their children to the faith. But while it is helpful to know the facts of faith in order to hand them on to our kids, there's something much more important. As Redemptorist Father Bernard Haring says in his book, *The Blessed Beatitudes,* "Theological research and reflection are important, but the heart of theology—the heart of Christian faith—is the experience of Christ's nearness."

Living in a family offers plenty of opportunities to practice that closeness:

- in compassion;
- in forgiveness;
- in willing sacrifice;
- in joy;
- in the beauty of nature;
- in unexpected laughter;
- in courage;
- in the faces of your family members;
- in the meals you share;
- as you worship or pray together as a family.

Were not our hearts burning within us while he was talking to us on the road?

Luke 24:32

August 5   Lives under construction

When a friend of mine was about nine years old her mother took her to the Art Institute of Chicago, where the two of them spent a day appreciating art and enjoying lunch in the museum's beautiful open-air courtyard restaurant. My friend was one of eight children, and it was unusual for her to have her mother all to herself like this. She asked, as only a nine-year-old can, "Mom, what are we doing here?"

To which her mother quickly responded, "We're building memories."

> *Remember these things, O Jacob, and Israel, for you are my servant; I formed you, you are my servant; O Israel, you will not be forgotten by me.*

Isaiah 44:21

August 6 Close to you

W hen I was growing up my school was visited one day by missionaries who had served in China. They encouraged us to think about what God's will might be for us, and I remember being both excited and scared by their challenge.

I didn't know where to begin. I figured in order to do God's will I'd have to go off and live a very different life, doing very different things, and being with very different people than I was with at the time. The more exotic my imaginings grew, the less likely I thought I would be able to respond well to my "vocation."

One Scripture passage has Moses telling the people (that is, you and me): "The command I enjoin on you today is not too mysterious and remote for you. It is not up in the sky...nor is it across the sea....No, it is something very near to you, already in your mouths and in your hearts; you have only to carry it out."

> *Now therefore, put away the foreign gods which are in your midst, and incline your hearts to the Lord, the God of Israel.*

Joshua 24:23

August 7   Living water

It's hot, muggy, and people are at each other's throats. There've been too many days in a row of heat with no relief. I get home from work and the kids are listless. They whine for no apparent reason. We don't even want to eat dinner.

We all go out in the backyard and sit with our feet in the kiddy pool, fresh cool water streaming in as we splash lazily in the shade. I remember what Jesus said about the kingdom of God being living water.

> *If you knew the gift of God, and who it is that is saying to you, "Give me a drink," you would have asked him, and he would have given you living water.*

John 4:10

August 8   Berry good

Summer is a time to experience miracles—like vine-ripened tomatoes in your salad, cherries in your mouth, blueberries on your cereal, or fresh peaches on your vanilla ice cream.

Invite your kids to take a long look at a plum, especially one that might still have its stem and a few leaves attached. Have them think of the soil, sun, rain and time that went into bringing forth this sweet, delicious taste. Then ask them to consider not only the One who created the plum but the amazing creatures who can taste and appreciate its goodness.

> *God said, "See, I have given you every plant yielding seed that is upon the face of all the earth, and every tree with seed in its fruit; you shall have them for food."*

Genesis 1:29

August 9 — Hard sayings

I saw a flyer for a presentation on "the hard sayings of Jesus." This would include, I assume, such difficult advice as "be not afraid," "the grain of wheat must die before it can bear good fruit," and "take up your cross and follow me."

My temptation is to give a kind of general nod to these difficult words but not take them seriously. Or, if I take them seriously, my next temptation is to simply write them off as impractical and not applicable to my life as a parent.

But experience continues to teach me that there is always more to what Jesus says than meets the eye. His teachings are worth mulling over—spending time with them and letting them sink in. Yet I also know that when I do come to a flash of understanding or appreciation of these gospel truths it's usually not from thinking about them but by living as faithfully as I can.

> *Make me to know your ways, O Lord; teach me your paths.*
>
> **Psalm 25:4**

August 10 — Image of God

I was once a high school teacher for a short period of time, and I tried to teach the kids about the beauty of the Lord's Prayer. One girl kept rolling her eyes, and as the class went on she grew more and more disturbed. I couldn't for the life of me figure out what was bothering her.

I caught up with her after class. "What's wrong, Mary?" I asked.

With her eyes misting, she blurted out, "Mr. McGrath, you wouldn't want to say that prayer if you had a father like mine!"

I was shocked and dismayed. We sat and talked for a long time. She told me how her father abused both her and her mother, ridiculing and belittling them whenever he could. She said that she had been able to hide her pain so that no one in the school knew what was going on. But when I tried to get her to think of God as a loving father it really bothered her.

For the first time in my life, I realized what Jesus meant when he said that it would be better to have a millstone tied around one's neck and be tossed into the sea than to ruin a child's image of God. Even now, I wonder if that girl has ever come to know God as a loving parent.

> *If any of you put a stumbling block before one of these little ones who believe in me, it would be better for you if a great millstone were hung around your neck and you were thrown into the sea.*

Mark 9:42

August 11   Momentum

It's my first day of vacation at Lake Time-to-Relax, and I'm a crazy man. I've been looking forward to this for a long time, but I can't seem to let go of the hectic pace I've carried with me from home. I feel as though I'm spoiling things for the entire family.

A man in the cabin next door senses how wired I am and laughs. He offers me an image that helps: "You know what happens to a person in a car that's going sixty miles an hour and abruptly stops? He keeps going right through the windshield. That's what you're going to do if you don't calm down."

I take a deep breath. If I give myself half a chance, I just might slow down in time to show up for my vacation.

> *Let a little water be brought, and wash your feet, and rest yourselves under the tree.*

Genesis 18:4

August 12   Marshmallows and starlight

My family is spending the week at my parents' cottage on a quiet lake in Michigan. The days have been generously long and lazy and we're coming "back to our senses." I notice it especially tonight, when we put together a campfire and roast marshmallows. I taste the sweetness of the marshmallow as if for the first time. I smell the evening breeze and it is crisp and clean. I think, "It can't get any better than this," but I haven't counted on the stars. After the fire dies down and we're heading back to the cottage, I walk out to the pier for one last breath of fresh air. Looking up I'm astounded and even disoriented by the array of stars like diamonds on black velvet.

God, you really know how to pour on the extravagance.

> *Is not God high in the heavens? See the highest stars, how lofty they are!*

Job 22:12

August 13   Sox game

I remember the first time I saw a major league baseball field. After tunneling through shadows and climbing grease-darkened stairs we came to the passageway leading to our seats. Suddenly I stepped out into the sunshine and a full view of the field. I'd never seen anything so green or so beautiful.

Years later, when they were about to tear down the old stadium, I brought my daughters to a White Sox game before it was too late. We sat in the right field bleachers where I'd sat with my family as a kid. I told the girls every story I could remember. There were the ladies in the neighborhood who would volunteer to take us kids on Ladies' Day when they got in free. There was the time Mom got hit in the hip by a batting practice home run, and when a greedy kid went to snatch the ball Mom stomped her foot on it and said, "I earned that one!" There was the double header with my uncle and cousins when we thought we'd won a thousand dollars but it turned out to be a thousand kosher dill pickles. And, finally, there was the game when I got the wind crushed out of me but still held onto that Harold Baines foul ball.

The girls and I had a great game cheering, singing and eating too much. Months later the stadium was gone but the experiences we had there will live on for generations.

Go, Sox.

> *On that day I will raise up the booth of David*
> *that is fallen, and repair its breaches, and raise*
> *up its ruins, and rebuild it as in the days of old.*
>
> **Amos 9:11**

August 14   Uncle Tom

My Uncle Tom was a bachelor who would buy us the toys our parents never would. If it was big, loud and exciting, Uncle Tom would sooner or later walk in with one for us. Tom's visit at Christmastime was more anticipated than Santa's.

We loved when he babysat for us because he had such interesting hobbies: playing tapes of old radio shows, taking target practice at old tin cans, and performing magic. He taught me how to make bright silk scarves disappear. He belonged to an archery club and would always take us to their annual roller skating party. (The first time we went I mistakenly thought we were going to be shooting bows and arrows on roller skates.)

Much of the rest of my life as a kid was staid and stable. Uncle Tom was different, odd, a wild card. Every child should have someone like him in the family.

The month had been turned for them from sorrow into gladness and from mourning into a holiday; that they should make them days of feasting and gladness, days for sending gifts of food to one another and presents to the poor.

Esther 9:22

August 15   No words to say

I see an old friend on the train and ask him how his kids are. I can see I hit a sore spot with him.

His son is having trouble finding himself. He's dropped out of school, moves from job to job, stays up late, and sleeps all day. He has little connection with the rest of the family. They've tried counselors, threats, heart-to-heart talks, and everything else they can think of. My friend, always proud of his own effectiveness on his job, is at his wits' end with his son.

I have no words of wisdom to share, only a recognition of how painful this situation must be for him. I know he's been a wonderful dad who has tried everything he can imagine to help his son. I sit mute before his suffering, hoping that author Garrison Keillor is right when he says, "Nothing you do for children is ever wasted."

The Lord is near to the brokenhearted, and saves the crushed in spirit.

Psalm 34:18

August 16   Bozo's accordionist

One summer I was in charge of my much younger brother and sister. I was sixteen and they were toddlers. I can't say I was ideal childcare material, but I learned one lesson that has come in handy: Life always goes better if you can make a game of it.

And so when nap time came and Marty and Peggy were reluctant to quit their fun and go to sleep, I got out my accordion and played one of their favorite songs, the "Grand Prize March" from the Bozo show. We would parade through the kitchen, dining room and living room. Then up the stairs we'd go, me playing that infernal instrument all the way to their beds, where they'd go to sleep…probably just to put an end to the racket.

*I will incline my ear to a proverb; I will solve
my riddle to the music of the harp.*

Psalm 49:4

August 17   Free gift, part 5

D o you realize that as a parent you need God's help and that all of life is a gift? That's Piety, another gift of the Holy Spirit.

*All things have been handed over to me by the
Father.*

Matthew 11:27

August 18   Unfinished business

I keep a postcard near my desk at work that features Michelangelo's statue of "The Young Slave." This is one of the series of statues that adorn the walkway toward his masterpiece, the statue of King David. Unlike David, who is complete down to the tiniest details, the slave statue is unfinished. It shows a young man trapped in stone, straining to get out.

I feel more like the slave than David—imperfect, incomplete, still in process. And so it's good for me to meditate occasionally on the beauty of the unfinished statue, on its power and promise. I realize that the master sculptor isn't finished with me yet, and somehow that makes me a better parent.

> *Did not he who made me in the womb make*
> *them? And did not one fashion us in the womb?*
>
> Job 31:15

August 19 — He said a mouthful

There's a message floating around the Internet. It's a collection of responses by children to the question, "What does love mean?"

There's one I found especially touching. Billy, who is four, said, "When someone loves you, the way they say your name is different. Your name is safe in their mouth."

I think back on how I sometimes bark out the names of my children in the heat of anger or frustration. For that moment, their names were not "safe" in my mouth. For these times I needed to apologize, to cleanse my palate.

God, help me to treat my children's names—and their tender hearts and souls—safely and with love.

> *I will give you the treasures of darkness and*
> *riches hidden in secret places, so that you may*
> *know that it is I, the Lord, the God of Israel,*
> *who call you by your name.*
>
> Isaiah 45:3

August 20   Good companions

When I was young the nuns would hand out holy cards with suggested "rules" of behavior for the summer as school let out. These rules included going to Mass each Sunday, seeing only "approved" movies, and hanging out only with "good companions."

Flash ahead about thirty years. On a long summer's evening my wife and I sit at a table with friends as our various children run around the yard together. We almost missed this opportunity; everyone's schedule was so packed we could hardly find a day we could all make it. But we persevered. As usual, the nuns were right about the value of those "good companions."

> *David went out to meet them and said to them,*
> *"If you have come to me in friendship, to help*
> *me, then my heart will be knit to you."*
>
> **1 Chronicles 12:17**

August 21   RSVP

We had just moved into a new parish. Our first child was only a few months old, and we were going to church sporadically at best. Then something small but significant happened. After one Mass a young woman in the parish introduced herself to us, chatted a while, and then invited us to her mother's home for an evening during the week for some tea and cake and conversation. There was a method to her madness. Her mother was the family life minister at our parish, and the two of them had made it their personal goal to reach out and welcome newcomers, especially young families.

It wasn't long before we were involved in a parish renewal program, had joined a faith sharing group that met for years in our house, and were committed to the parish community.

I think back and shudder at how much we would have missed if that woman had not issued her invitation or we had begged off because we were too busy.

> *Go therefore into the main streets, and invite*
> *everyone you find to the wedding banquet.*
>
> **Matthew 22:9**

August 22   The universe as puzzle, part 2

I t's the night before my older daughter is heading off to her first year of college. My heart is aching. There are no words to say. Up in the attic getting some luggage for her, I notice the circle puzzle that was put away many years ago. I bring it downstairs, and that night the girls humor their mother and me and agree to put the puzzle together one more time.

The girls make the popcorn and set up a card table. We gather around the puzzle with its starscape center and rings of animals and landscapes and people from around the world. It used to take us all night to put it together, but we finish the puzzle in no time at all. My girls have learned their way around the universe. They are ready to go.

> *The Lord will open for you his rich storehouse,*
> *the heavens, to give the rain of your land in its*
> *season and to bless all your undertakings.*
>
> **Deuteronomy 28:12**

August 23   Anger revisited

T he mom was angry with her son. They exchanged harsh words and it escalated. She lashed out after a particularly stinging comment on his part, bringing up an incident from years past.

Immediately she wished she could grab her words from mid air and swallow them down. She had thought she was over that past incident and had forgiven him completely, but apparently not.

After they both cooled down and apologies were offered and received on both sides, she sat and mused about how she'd broken her own rule and brought up an old issue in a new argument. She realized that forgiveness is a process, and that in this case the process was not yet finished.

Now, in addition to retracing the path of forgiveness for her son's past transgression, she had to walk the rocky path of trying to forgive herself for her present one.

> **John the Baptizer appeared in the wilderness, proclaiming a baptism of repentance for the forgiveness of sins.**
>
> **Mark 1:4**

August 24   Blind spots

W e were ahead at a basketball game at the school gym. One of my neighbor's sons was taunting the opponents. I was shocked. My neighbor was sitting right there, watching it happen. I knew the dad would never participate in such behavior himself, but there was his son acting like a jerk and the dad was totally blind to it.

I am often amazed when I'm with very aware parents who are nonetheless blind to an annoying or troubling trait in their child.

It's clear to everyone else that this child could use some parental guidance in overcoming this problem, but the parents seem oblivious to it.

I walk out of the gym, shaking my head. I'm sure glad you and I don't have any blind spots as parents.

Right?

> *But whoever hates another believer is in the darkness, walks in the darkness, and does not know the way to go, because the darkness has brought on blindness.*
>
> **1 John 2:11**

August 25   Special delivery

A lot of us parents have trouble putting our feelings into words. We like to do things with our kids, and that means a lot to them. But they also want and need to hear explicitly from us just how much we care for them.

Here's a tip: Put it in writing. Take a few minutes to write a letter to each of your children to say what's on your mind. But stick to the positive and concentrate on your feelings. I have found this method to be a great way to convey some of the depth of what I'm feeling for my kids at various ages—when they accomplished something great, when they were going through hard times, when they had done something kind and generous. Don't worry. You'll find the words. Just take the time.

And if you think these letters won't really mean much to your child, imagine a morning when you are rummaging around in your sock drawer and come upon a packet of letters to you from your dad. Would you just toss them aside?

My children didn't.

*My child, be attentive to my words, incline your
ear to my sayings.*

Proverbs 4:20

August 26   Heroes

Have you told your kids who your heroes are? Today
might be a good time to do so. It's a great way to let them
know what matters most to you and what you aspire to
be. Make sure to include family members from the past whom you
admire and want to emulate. It will give them a sense that they are
part of a larger story and that life is a heroic adventure.

> *Then the Lord said to Jacob, "Return to the land
> of your ancestors and to your kindred, and I
> will be with you."*

Genesis 31:3

August 27   Make friends with silence

A friend of mine is a monk, so I consider him to be an expert
on silence. He says that what scares people most about silence is how *noisy* it really is. What happens when people
eliminate noise from their lives, he reports, is that they come to
hear the sounds of nature or the breathing of others around them
or even what's going on in their own heads.

I don't know about you, but I've got quite a committee up in my
noggin. It seems that the committee is always in session, trying to
change, fix and control the world (and especially my children). It
hasn't been very successful over the years, but that doesn't stop the
meeting from continuing without adjournment. Yet I have also
come to recognize that silence is one of the places where I meet

169

God. Silence is healing, restorative. It is one of the languages God uses to communicate with humans.

Silence may take some getting used to, but it is a good antidote to the noisiness of our world. Help your kids develop a taste for silence as a natural part of life.

> *Then Moses and the levitical priests spoke to all*
> *Israel, saying: Keep silence and hear, O Israel!*
> *This very day you have become the people of the*
> *Lord your God.*

Deuteronomy 27:9

August 28   Getting even

The younger daughter was angry. Her older sister had hurt her feelings. Now she wanted, more than anything in the world, to get even. But she was smaller and not yet as clever, and she knew she would get in trouble if she did the things she wanted to do.

"What are you feeling?" asked her mom.

"Angry!"

"Is that all?" pushed the mom, waiting while her daughter looked around inside.

"No. I'm sad too."

"Can you tell your sister that you're sad?"

"She'll make fun of me."

"Maybe not."

Slowly, reluctantly, the little girl said, "Okay. I'll try."

And off she went in the hope of getting what she originally wanted.

She discovered something much better.

Do not say, "I will do to others as they have
done to me. I will pay them back for what they
have done."

Proverbs 24:29

August 29   Chores

A friend of mine was telling me how his dad made chores
fun. They had nine kids, so even unloading the week's groceries from the car could be quite a project. "Dad would
have all of us who were old enough in the kitchen at the ready.
He'd stand in the doorway with the bags of groceries and fling
items one-by-one at us. As each of us caught one, that person
would have to scramble to put it away and get back in line before
the next item came his or her way.

"Dad threw everything—pickle jars, ice cream, eggs," my friend
remembered. "You had to be ready. More than one can or bottle
would end up on the floor, and we'd all laugh, but we had those
groceries put away in no time."

Chores are good for kids. It teaches them all sorts of lessons, including that we all need to do our share to get along in life. But
chores don't have to be drudgery. It's all in the spirit with which we
approach the task.

> *And also their neighbors, from as far away as Is-*
> *sachar and Zebulun and Naphtali, came bring-*
> *ing food on donkeys, camels, mules, and oxen—*
> *abundant provisions of meal, cakes of figs, clus-*
> *ters of raisins, wine, oil, oxen, and sheep, for*
> *there was joy in Israel.*

1 Chronicles 12:40

171

August 30   Night watchman

There are times I awaken late at night and walk through the house checking that all is well. As I stand in the midst of the living room, I am surrounded by the spirit of all the friends who drop by regularly to visit. I look at the dining room table and feel the presence of all the relatives who join our family at Thanksgiving or other family feasts. I glance at my daughters' bedrooms and think of the kids who used to run in there to play with their Barbies and board games. I sit at the kitchen table and recall how the Advent wreath glows there in December and how the homework gets spread out there almost every night. There are echoes of music from many eras throughout the house and aromas from baking bread and cookies lingering in the air.

In other words, I see your fingerprints, God, all over everything.

Did not my hand make all these things?

Acts 7:50

August 31   Parenting lesson

When you're feeling overwhelmed by a parenting challenge, take three steps: 1) ask God for help, 2) do the "next right thing" in front of you, 3) get out of the way. The first step is self-explanatory. The second moves you from paralysis to productive action. It is based on the idea that while we often cannot know all the things we need to do to resolve a situation we usually can decide what is the next right thing to do. The third step is based on the fact that God works in surprising ways. Often, because I am so set on my own preconceived notions of how things ought to turn out, I end up being the one who is blocking the change that needs to happen.

Happy are those who make the Lord their trust.

Psalm 40:4

September 1   Labor days

While visiting a Trappistine Monastery in Iowa, I followed my nose to their wonderful homemade candy factory. At the entrance to one of the rooms where they make their heavenly chocolate mints I spied a sign that said, "All work is holy."

I complain at least once in a while about my work, and yet I've come to appreciate over the years how important my work is to me. Not only does it allow me to contribute to supporting my family and household, but there is also a spirituality of work that deepens my faith and love for God.

At Mass the priest asks God to accept our offerings, which are "fruit of the vine and the work of human hands." What a partnership: nature's bounty and our efforts, combined to make our gift to God. Seeing our work in such a light helps avoid the temptations of materialism, workaholism, blind ambition or no ambition.

Talk to your kids about work this week and let them know one reward you find in the work you're called to do. (If you can't think of one, maybe it's time to dust off the resume or get out the classifieds.)

> *The point is this: the one who sows sparingly*
> *will also reap sparingly, and the one who sows*
> *bountifully will also reap bountifully.*
> 2 Corinthians 9:6

September 2   Fresh start

The bell rings at the beginning of each school year, and we all come running—parents and children alike.

Thank you, God, for fresh beginnings. New school supplies, new shoes, new chances. Help me to cherish these tender new sprouts of hope rising up in my kids and in me.

You give us a fresh start every year and every day, Lord. Help me to let go of the past and live in the grace I'm given today.

In the beginning was the Word, and the Word was with God, and the Word was God.

John 1:1

September 3   Watch my children well

Have you seen how he furrows his brow? He'll do that, you know, when he's puzzling over a question. Sometimes his questions go deep, so be prepared.

Do you know that when she's bossy she's really just afraid? She truly is a kind and loving child, if you'll but give her a moment to soothe herself.

Have you caught how imaginative they can be? How freely their minds range and roam when encouraged and allowed, inventing new worlds that will bring you delight?

Have you seen? Oh, watch them please. Watch them closely and you'll see what wonderful children you will be watching.

But even the hairs of your head are all counted. Do not be afraid; you are of more value than many sparrows.

Luke 12:7

September 4   Check the directions

I was once reading the true account of an adventure when I came across the line, "Having lost our way, we redoubled our efforts." That actually sounded to me like a surefire way to get all the more lost.

Rather than just "redoubling our efforts" at the beginning of a new school season, it's good for us parents to take a break at this time of year—not only to get some rest but also to get some clarity. The kids are in school, at least for a few hours a day, and we can take the opportunity to step back and notice where our actions might be out of sync with our values. And if they are we can look inside ourselves to find our way.

> *I have gone astray like a lost sheep; seek out your servant, for I do not forget your commandments.*
>
> **Psalms 119:176**

September 5   Keeping watch

I remember spying on you from the kitchen window while you spent joyful mornings playing games in your turtle-shaped sandbox.

I loved to watch you with your building blocks, putting one ever so softly atop the other, building towers that were impossibly high. And as you played with your crayons and finger paints I saw that you were totally unaware of time, totally awake to the moment.

Tonight I watch Farragut High School's newest art teacher lean over her lesson plans with light in her eyes. A smile erupts as you dream up yet another way to charm life-hardened high schoolers into letting the little kid inside themselves come out and play once again.

As you plan the hours go by and you remain unaware of time and awake to this new moment. And I have another memory to cherish.

*Whoever welcomes one such child in my name
welcomes me, and whoever welcomes me welcomes not me but the one who sent me.*

Mark 9:37

September 6   Why did Jesus come?

I saw a bumper sticker that said, "Jesus is coming again. Everybody look busy!"

This made me laugh on a couple of counts. First, it ex-
presses one of the great maladies of our day—that being busy (or
at least looking busy) somehow implies moral superiority over just
being.

Secondly, the bumper sticker confuses why Jesus became human
in the first place. If you ask people why Jesus came to live among
us, most say something like "to die for our sins," "to teach us right
from wrong," "to redeem us from bondage to sin." But Jesus came
for more than that. Those things merely evened the score and got
us back to a level playing field. Let's let Jesus tell us in his own
words why he came: "I came that you might have life and have it
abundantly."

That's what parenting is about too, isn't it? We don't just want
our children to avoid bad things or merely to survive life, we want
them to flourish and prosper and grow. We want them to have life
and have it abundantly.

Thank you, Jesus!

*I came that they may have life, and have it
abundantly.*

John 10:10

September 7   Lost and alone?

G od, in my uncertainty as a parent, fear of doing harm to those I love paralyzes me. Even minor problems seem to be more than I can handle. It seems everything I do makes the situation worse.

I have one thing to hang on to. I remember your words to the apostles and your words to me, "I will be with you all days." Lord, this is a day I really need you near.

> *Reside in this land as an alien, and I will be*
> *with you, and will bless you; for to you and to*
> *your descendants I will give all these lands, and*
> *I will fulfill the oath that I swore to your father*
> *Abraham.*

Genesis 26:3

September 8   Tough lessons

R esiliency is more than just coping," said the speaker at a conference I attended last week. "Resiliency is discovering gifts within the tough time we're having."

She was quick to add that the tough times may not be any sort of gift and may, in fact, be horrible. But those with resilience seem to find within difficult situations some gifts that put the suffering in a wider context.

That happened with my mother and her sister, Nora, when Nora was very ill before she died. My mother went to see Nora most days. They enjoyed spending time together. At the time my mom told me, "You know, it's just so wonderful to have this time where we can be together so closely, to just share what's on our minds, to laugh—and we do laugh at the goofiest things—and to cry." The two obviously gained strength and comfort from each other. They found resiliency in this most difficult time.

Children can practice resiliency if we first help them acknowledge that their situation is indeed difficult. If we try to make light of the situation or dismiss it, it can seem to negate a part of them or deny their experience. But if we can acknowledge, "Yeah, this is a tough situation," then we can also add, "but you are strong, and I wonder what you're going to do about it or learn from it." Once they rise to the occasion they may just find the gifts that were hidden in the tough times they have made it through.

> *But the more they were oppressed, the more they*
> *multiplied and spread.*
>
> **Exodus 1:12**

September 9 — Buddy system

I ran a ten-mile race last week for the first time in my life. "I never knew you were a runner," said a surprised friend when he heard of my accomplishment. Others asked how I'd done it. I told them, "A guy in the neighborhood invited me to run with him on Saturday mornings. We added a mile a week and before you know it I was ready for the ten-mile run."

After explaining this a few times, I came to realize how helpful it is to have companions on the journey. Our kids need companions too. That's one reason it's good to connect them with a community of fellow believers. It's also why we should do more than just urge them to be good or practice their faith. Rather, we need to tell them about our relationship with God and invite them to "run along with us."

There's an old joke told by Catholics. A man asks a priest. "Father, how often should I make my son go to confession?" The wise priest smiles and says, "Oh, just bring him along whenever you go."

> *May your friends be like the sun as it rises in its might.*
>
> Judges 5:31

September 10   Keep an eraser handy

I was giving a talk at a parish in Massachusetts and the participants were swapping parenting tips. One idea especially caught my attention that I think many parents could put to good use. A woman told how her sister's family has the practice of "erasing" something they just said. If they say something stupid or mean in the heat of an argument, they stop the action, ask forgiveness on the spot, and say, "I erase the last twenty seconds of our conversation." She said that this little practice has stopped a lot of conversations from going downhill in her sister's family.

The woman then told how she had written an ill-advised letter to her son in college. As soon as she dropped it in the mailbox she regretted sending it. She called her son and asked if she could erase the letter. He called her back when he received it and ripped it up (unopened) over the phone.

> *Then Saul said, "I have done wrong; come back, my son David, for I will never harm you again, because my life was precious in your sight today; I have been a fool, and have made a great mistake."*
>
> 1 Samuel 26:21

September 11   Remembering

Today's date will forever stand as a solemn day in our collective memory. It is a day when a great evil was visited on the world. It's a number—"9/11"—our children will always know the meaning of. They likely will be able to answer immediately when asked, "Where were you when you first heard the news?"

When the great tragedy struck, we all turned immediately and naturally to our faith for strength, meaning and direction. Our prayers and offerings of assistance were our way of transforming our pain into something creative, life giving and life affirming.

Maybe we need to get back to that place on this date each year. Gather your family together today—to remember, to pray, to decide who is most in need of your help now.

> *Give ear to my words, O Lord; give heed to my sighing. Listen to the sound of my cry, my King and my God, for to you I pray.*
>
> **Psalm 5:1**

September 12   Prayer partners

Put the names of your family members on separate slips of paper and put them in a bowl. Then have each member of your family pick out one name apiece and make that person his or her special "prayer partner" that month.

That way everyone in your family will know for sure that there is someone praying specifically for him or her. That's a real blessing, a concrete comfort, a welcome security blanket.

> *Pray without ceasing.*
>
> **1 Thessalonians 5:17**

September 13   Transform or transmit

I heard Franciscan priest Richard Rohr say, "If we do not transform our pain, we will always transmit it."

I see how that happens in my family. Sometimes I have a bad day at work and feel belittled, disappointed, ashamed. I try to deny it, to plow ahead with life, but when the smallest slight or back talk happens at home I lash out with the full fury of the storm raging inside of me.

God, why couldn't I have simply borne the full depth of my feelings and given it to you to transform?

> *The wilderness and the dry land shall be glad,*
> *the desert shall rejoice and blossom; like the crocus it shall blossom abundantly.*

Isaiah 35:1-2

September 14   Story in progress

O nce a pond of time," you wrote in large crooked letters. Thus you had begun the storybook you wanted to write when you were six. I spied it on your bedstand one night after you drifted off to sleep.

> *That time remains a pond,*
> *from which I drink deep*
> *of pure and innocent faith,*
> *a pond of memories,*
> *of fierce and protective love.*

Tomorrow you leave for college two states away, a young woman, off to make your future and find your fortune, to finally write the story of your life.

The earth was a formless void and darkness cov-
ered the face of the deep, while a wind from
God swept over the face of the waters.

Genesis 1:2

September 15   Free gift, part 7

Have you felt awe, perhaps the first day you held your child in your arms? That's Fear of the Lord, the seventh and final gift of the Holy Spirit.

Parenting begins in awe, which means it begins as a sacred relationship. Recapture the awe; practice it; nurture it. Fear of the Lord is not being afraid of God. It is a gift that is rightfully yours.

Make a joyful noise to the Lord, all the earth;
break forth into joyous song and sing praises.

Psalm 98:4

September 16   Obey your thirst

I was reading the account of Jesus and the Samaritan woman at the well. It dawned on me that while Jesus asked the woman for something to drink, the story was all about the *woman's* thirst. Through the travails of five husbands she had obviously been thirsting for something more than she had found. As the country western song puts it, she'd spent her life "lookin' for love in all the wrong places." Jesus told her of a better way to quench her thirst, a way that was eternally satisfying.

I take great comfort in seeing that Jesus is more interested in my thirst than in my sins. Life can encourage me to ignore my thirst—to keep on pushing harder and harder at the many duties involved in being a parent, spouse, worker, neighbor, parishioner and so forth. Ignoring my thirst is often what leads me to errant ways. I get resentful and angry, confused and empty. Meanwhile, Jesus sits at the well, inviting me to pay attention to both my physical needs and my deeper longing for God. He is always ready to give me a long, cool drink of living water.

> *When the poor and needy seek water, and there*
> *is none, and their tongue is parched with thirst,*
> *I the Lord will answer them, I the God of Israel*
> *will not forsake them.*

Isaiah 41:17

September 17   Simple gifts

The retired man down the block loves it when little kids stop and talk to him. He's crusty, a tough guy of sorts. But not when the kids come calling. He sits on his front porch, all smiles and grins, and asks them, "Hey, whatcha up to, pardner?" The kids spot a softie and crawl all over him.

His own grown sons have children, and my heart delights to watch my neighbor and his spry wife out playing tag and hide-n'-seek with them in their back yard.

There's a time during the Mass when we're invited to place our "gifts" on the altar—those things we did during the week that we would like to offer in gratitude for God's gift of life. I think of my neighbor. He doesn't get to church too often, so mentally I place upon the altar all the times he sits and jokes with the kids on the block or with his grandchildren. Those precious moments belong there. When it's time for Communion I take the host and enjoy the sweetness it contains. "Unless you become like little children, you will not enter the kingdom of God," Jesus said. My neighbor is showing me the way to do that.

> *The righteous are generous and keep giving.*

Psalm 37:21

September 18   Faithfully yours

It's in God's nature to be true and faithful. This is the good news that Jesus revealed to us: that God is like a loving parent. God's nature is to offer love and mercy, no matter what we have done or where we have strayed.

There will be times when we parents are less than faithful in our lives. Some may think our sins should disqualify us from the chance to get back on track with our kids or back in God's good graces. But God doesn't share that view.

Saint Paul wrote to Timothy: "If we are unfaithful, God remains faithful, for he cannot deny himself." All we need to do is turn to God with our whole heart. And we can do that anytime, anywhere. As the bumper sticker says, "It's never too late to have a good day."

> *God is faithful, and he will not let you be tested*
> *beyond your strength, but with the testing he*
> *will also provide the way out so that you may*
> *be able to endure it.*

1 Corinthians 10:13

September 19   Check your troubles

When my older daughter, Judy, was having a rough time with her college schoolwork I realized there was no direct help I could offer. I did tell her that when I found myself overwhelmed with worry about many things, I simply imagine God sitting on a big throne and into his lap I put all my worries.

I wasn't sure my words did any good, but at least I had tried to fulfill my parental responsibility.

More than a year later, when I was going through a difficult time myself, this same daughter came home from school with a shoebox for me. "Open it," she said. Inside was a statue she had made. It was a statue of Mary, Jesus' mother, seated with her arms circling her lap, holding a little basket full of black stones. "This is for your worries, Dad," Judy told me.

Since then, there have been few days that I haven't placed a stone or two in Mary's lap, freeing me to stop my worrying and do what I need to do.

> *Bear one another's burdens, and in this way you will fulfill the law of Christ.*
>
> **Galatians 6:2**

September 20   Trust

I can believe that God exists but still have a hard time trusting God when difficult times come my way. Here's a story about trusting, though it means I'll have to tell you about something foolish I did.

I was coming home from a men's group meeting where we had been talking about trusting God. On the way home I saw an obviously drunk young man stumbling around in a fairly dangerous neighborhood. He was in the wrong place at the wrong time and was bound to get hurt. When he put out his thumb for a ride, I naively told him, "Sure, hop in." He ranted and raved drunkenly for a while, but I didn't get worried until I heard the click of his switchblade knife. He leaned toward me and held the knife to my neck. I was terrified. The words I had spoken about trust just a half hour earlier rang hollow in my heart. But I was at a crossroads. In my heart, I made an act of will. I decided to simply trust in God.

My fear melted away. My anxiety disappeared. I didn't know what the outcome would be, but I trusted God nonetheless. As if by magic, a change came over the young man next to me. He leaned back, folded the knife, and put it back in his jacket pocket. At the next stoplight, I pulled the car to the curb and told him he could get a great cup of coffee at the diner right there. He looked at me with bleary eyes, nodded, and then without a word he left the car. I proceeded home with two amazing gifts: a deeply intense appreciation for being alive and a recognition that no matter what comes my way, trusting God is always an option.

Now I need to figure out how to teach this lesson to my daughters without having them do something as foolish as I did.

*In God, whose word I praise, in God I trust; I
am not afraid; what can flesh do to me?*

Psalm 56:4

September 21   It can't hurt

Dorothy Day, a great American holy woman now being considered for sainthood, would often pray for unknown people on the verge of suicide. She never knew whether her prayers were helpful to these strangers, but she believed enough to continue the practice her entire life.

Scientists are now proving what believers have known all along: that praying for people—even if they don't know you're praying for them—can have beneficial effects on them.

Spend a spare moment today praying for someone who desperately needs your prayers. Invite your children to get in the habit of doing likewise.

The Lord hears when I call to him.

Psalm 4:3

September 22   How to be "heartily sorry"

O my God, I am heartily sorry." These were the opening words to the act of contrition I was taught as a kid.

Being heartily sorry takes three steps: 1) admit you did wrong, 2) accept the consequences, 3) change your tune. It takes guts to acknowledge when you've made a serious mistake. But if we know that God is eager to forgive and welcome us back into a right relationship, then such admissions are easier. This same knowledge also makes us more willing to accept the consequences that come from our misdeed.

What comes next, however, is most important if we parents hope to avoid further harm to our children. We need to change the behaviors that led to our wrongdoing. We need to live a new kind of life. If it was a small matter, the changes we need to make may be small. If it was a major wrong, we need to be willing to accept major change and live a new way. That's the way to be sorry with all your heart, or "heartily sorry."

> *The sacrifice acceptable to God is a broken spirit; a broken and contrite heart, O God, you will not despise.*
>
> **Psalm 51:17**

September 23   The critic

A ny fool can criticize, and most of them do." So says a wise bumper sticker.

I have become aware of just how much of my day I spend in a negative manner. I try to make myself feel better by putting others down. But this is about as effective as trying to make myself healthier by eating junk food. Eventually it'll make me sick.

And the kids might catch the disease from me.

Or how can you say to your neighbor, "Friend,
let me take out the speck in your eye," when you
yourself do not see the log in your own eye? You
hypocrite, first take the log out of your own eye,
and then you will see clearly to take the speck
out of your neighbor's eye.

Luke 6:42

September 24   Pollyannish? Not!

Many people I meet tell me they are worried about their adult children and grandchildren. They worry because the younger generation is not regularly practicing their faith. I tell them that the best thing they can do is to deepen their own faith and trust that all things work out in the end. This is not blind pollyannishness. It is a recognition that God has ways of reaching people beyond what we can know or understand.

Our practice of faith as parents can be one way that God reaches others. As Franciscan Father Richard Rohr says, "We must believe in such a way that we give hope and meaning to the next generation."

We know that all things work together for good
for those who love God, who are called accord-
ing to his purpose.

Romans 8:28

September 25   Accepting forgiveness

Peter and Judas each needed to be forgiven. Peter, though painfully aware of his sin, opened his heart and accepted forgiveness. Judas couldn't do it. His heart remained locked. He self-destructed.

One of the things we parents need to teach our children is how to accept forgiveness.

> *At that moment the cock crowed for the second time. Then Peter remembered that Jesus had said to him, "Before the cock crows twice, you will deny me three times." And he broke down and wept.*

Mark 14:72

September 26   Have faith in your faith

I once heard author Philip Yancey tell how he learned the value of "doubting my doubts as much as I doubt my faith." I was interviewing him for *U.S. Catholic* magazine when he said, "Why should I act as if my doubts are so on target and what I believe in is bogus?" He described faith as a bulls-eye with concentric rings around it. In the center, things are very sharp and clear. Issues may get fuzzier as you move to the edges.

"Love one another as I have loved you" is a bulls-eye for me. When I focus on that and give myself over to that truth—practically and materially in my daily, ordinary life with my children— then my doubts fade away and the truth becomes clearer. I know it in my bones.

> *Ask in faith, never doubting, for the one who doubts is like a wave of the sea, driven and tossed by the wind.*

James 1:6

September 27   Laborers

J esus said, "The harvest is great, but the laborers are few." He was moved with pity for the crowds because "they were troubled and abandoned, like sheep without a shepherd."

So what kind of "laborers" was Jesus hoping would emerge? Mostly, he was looking for people who were willing to not only *proclaim* the good news but to actually *be* the good news for others. He was hoping for people who could—through their words and actions—heal, welcome, encourage, and lift up the hearts of those who were troubled and abandoned.

As parents we get the chance to labor for our children every day, but especially when they feel troubled and abandoned.

> **There the wicked cease from troubling, and**
> **there the weary are at rest.**

Job 3:17

September 28   Feed my lambs

A t Mass each week in my parish the young children from kindergarten through third grade are led out of the main church for their own special Liturgy of the Word. I love to see them, so innocent and eager, drift up toward the altar and gather for their blessing before proceeding off to their story room.

I remember my own kids at that age and how eager they were to hear the biblical stories and to make sense out of the religion we were introducing to them. I look closely at the young boys and girls now, knowing that seeds of faith are being planted in them, just as it was in my children.

Today's youth will surely need faith to make it through the world they will inherit tomorrow. Who knows? The saint we have all been waiting for may be skipping through church right before our very eyes.

Truly I tell you, unless you change and become like children, you will never enter the kingdom of heaven.

Matthew 18:3

September 29   Less is more

We went to see the most hyped movie of the summer. Everyone had raved about it, but by the time I got to see it I knew all the twists of the plot. There was no way it could live up to my expectations. I felt cheated.

There used to be a comedy skit about how to find more satisfaction in life and relationships. The punch line was "Lower your expectations!" The intention was to be ironic, but I find some true wisdom in the concept. Often I build up a situation in my mind, thinking that it has to be wonderful. It might be a weekend plan, or a birthday party for one of the kids, or even just some time alone with a family member. If I let my expectations grow out of hand, I'm sure to be disappointed. Yet if I just let a situation unfold without any big expectations, there's usually a very simple joy available for the taking.

You have looked for much, and, lo, it came to little.

Haggai 1:9

September 30   Yikes!

Families had gathered up at church for a potluck dinner, games and music. My daughters were still little kids, or so I thought until the music started. I guess I'd seen this kind of dancing on television or movies, but I'd never seen *my* darlings involved in it.

Boys and girls were gyrating and waving their arms and moving their bodies in ways that seemed more appropriate for a cheap motel than a parish gym. Parents of older kids laughed knowingly. "It's a shock, isn't it, the first time you see your kids acting like teenagers?" they said.

Indeed it was. Upon further reflection I realized this was a rite of passage. They weren't doing anything my generation and other generations haven't done. What I had reacted to was not the dancing but the fact that my daughters had reached a momentous time in their life—for them and for me.

> *No one puts new wine into old wineskins; otherwise, the wine will burst the skins, and the wine is lost, and so are the skins; but one puts new wine into fresh wineskins.*

Mark 2:22

October 1   Sharing faith

For years my family belonged to a faith-sharing group that gathered weekly in our home. We met at our house because we were the ones who had the youngest children and could not afford weekly babysitting. This turned out to be a major blessing for the girls.

Our kids would help us get the chairs ready, the coasters out, the cookies or cake on the coffee table, and the coffee cups on the side table. Then our friends would gather as my daughters were going to bed, so they got to greet and say goodnight to our fellow parishioners.

One night, about a half hour into the meeting, I could still hear my daughters gabbing in their bedroom. It dawned on me then that they could hear us too, and I was delighted. It warmed my heart to know my daughters were drifting off to sleep to the sound of adults looking at their daily lives and finding ample evidence of the presence of God.

> ***Let anyone with ears to hear listen!***
> **Luke 14:35**

October 2   Together

When I was first married I used to dream of owning my own Chicago-style hot dog stand. I liked the idea of running my own business. I knew that it would involve long hours, low pay and unending responsibility, but it was my dream. (I know, other people dream of finding a cure for cancer, but—what the heck—it was *my* dream!)

Instead of opening a hot dog stand, we had kids. That too, we discovered, involves long hours, low pay and unending responsibility. One of the tricks my wife and I used to help us rise to the challenge of raising children was to think about it as a family business. We knew that the early years would demand great investment of time and energy and sacrifice, but we figured that every effort we put in early would reap rewards down the line, and that has proven to be true beyond our most fervent hope.

Rather than owning McGrath's Chicago Dogs, we now have the McGrath Family. Fortunately, we found we could cut the mustard and do it with relish!

> *The good person out of the good treasure of the heart produces good.*
>
> **Luke 6:45**

October 3   Appreciate the harvest

Human minds are funny. It's easy to be keenly aware of all the things we've done wrong or left uncompleted. Yet we can easily miss or forget all the success we have achieved. This unhealthy pattern saps joy from life. Worse, we can pass our attitudes and habits on to our kids. If we don't appreciate the positive things we have done, neither will they.

So stop today and recognize your own accomplishments. Don't forget to recognize some of the "kinder, gentler" things you do, like spending time reading stories to your children. It's very empowering to realize just how accomplished you are as a parent.

> *You shall observe the festival of harvest, of the first fruits of your labor, of what you sow in the field. You shall observe the festival of ingathering at the end of the year, when you gather in from the field the fruit of your labor.*
>
> **Exodus 23:16**

October 4   Follow whom?

J esus said we must be like a grain of wheat that falls to the
ground and dies and then produces much fruit. I know quite
clearly the places in my life I need to be willing to die. I just
don't want to do it.

For example, I often realize that my family could use more of my
attention, more of my time, more of me, but I'd rather keep doing
the Sunday crossword puzzle or maybe some reading from the office.

Jesus, I would much rather admire you than follow you.

> *Very truly, I tell you, unless a grain of wheat*
> *falls into the earth and dies, it remains just a*
> *single grain; but if it dies, it bears much fruit.*
>
> **John 12:24**

October 5   Communion in the park

O ne October fifth, many years ago, the pope came to my
home town. My family was given two tickets to the
papal Mass in Grant Park along Chicago's beautiful
lakefront, and my mother and I were the two available to attend.

The tickets we had would have allowed us to sit in the restrict-
ed area right near the altar. But as we tried to get there, the swarms
of people clamoring for the front seats seemed repugnant to my
mother. We gave the tickets away and drifted off across the street
to sit with picnickers in a grove of ancient elms.

Mom felt more comfortable there, out of the limelight, off to the
side, sitting close to the earth among good, simple people who had
ridden busses a long distance to join the festivities. It was a perfect
autumn day.

We could hear the singing of the hymns and we joined in. The preaching was indistinct where we sat, and instead we listened to the sound of the birds and the wind through the trees. At Communion time it took a long time for the Eucharistic ministers to make it back to where we were gathered, and people would take their own host, break it, and share it with those hovering around the edges. Mom broke hers, gave me a sliver, and put the rest in her purse for Dad.

This is the faith my parents nurtured in me: strong, immediate, generous, practical and real. I hope I can do the same for my children.

> *This is the bread that came down from heaven, not like that which your ancestors ate, and they died. But the one who eats this bread will live forever.*
>
> **John 6:58**

October 6   Hungry

I find myself standing in front of the open refrigerator and wondering how long I'd been there. My daughter asks, "Whatcha' lookin' for Dad?" I answer, "I really don't know."

There are times I get hungry but nothing really appeals to me. If I try to eat, I remain unsatisfied. I think there's a spiritual parallel. There are times when there's a hunger inside that seems too great to be sated. Or as my friend Kevin says, "There's an itchin' in your heart and you can't quite scratch it."

Only God can fill that emptiness, satisfy that hunger, scratch that itch. The worst thing to do is to eat what will not satisfy— whether it's loading our life with work, watching sports obsessively, eating compulsively, or any number of other poor substitutes. Sometimes the best we can do is merely live with the hunger and patiently open our heart to God.

You have given him his heart's desire, and have
not withheld the request of his lips.

Psalm 21:2

October 7   Interwoven mysteries

A mom sits at the kitchen table as her three kids come in from school. One child runs in with yet another A+ on a test. Another hangs his head as he hands over his test score—a D. And he had studied so very hard! The third child can't remember if she had any tests returned from the teacher but says, "Y'know what, Mom? I saw a butterfly coming out of a cocoon on the playground and we fed it grass and...."

This mom, her emotions whipsawing moment by moment, wonders how to take all this in and, more important, how to respond to it. She thinks of the Rosary she had been saying just before the kids came home. The decades were neatly separated into the joyful, sorrowful, and glorious mysteries. But life is not that organized. The mysteries come in a jumble—joyful, sorrowful, glorious—all at once. She knows they came that way for Jesus and his mother too.

God, give us parents hearts big enough to embrace everything that happens to our children today. Help us to hold all these things, not be overwhelmed by any of them, to give each its due, and to be present and prepared for the next moment of life.

> *And the child's father and mother were amazed*
> *at what was being said about him. Then Simeon*
> *blessed them and said to his mother Mary, "This*
> *child is destined for the falling and the rising of*
> *many in Israel, and to be a sign that will be op-*
> *posed so that the inner thoughts of many will be*
> *revealed—and a sword will pierce your own*
> *soul too."*

Luke 2:33-35

October 8 — Radical trust

The clock radio came on this morning, waking us to news of threats, counter-threats and war. As a parent, of course, my mind went to worries about my children's safety and my heart was gripped with fear. As I lay in bed I prayed for the strength to do what parents must always learn to do: let go.

I learned a lesson about letting go from Wendy Wright's masterful book, *Sacred Dwelling: A Spirituality of Family Life*. She says that for parents, letting go involves "radical faith." She is not talking about a fair-weather faith that assumes only good things will happen to our kids. Rather, it's a faith that "somehow God's presence is available to us even in the mysteries of human suffering and death…. This kind of radical trust in an accompanying God is what allows us to let go."

> *Do not fear those who kill the body but cannot kill the soul.*

Matthew 10:28

October 9 — Big John

I was at a wake the other night. As always, stories were told and memories were cherished. It's important for people of faith to report the "good news" according to the life of their loved one who has died. One young man, Dolph, said he'd always remember his uncle, Big John or "Uncle Bigs," for organizing the annual family picnic and the elaborate games for the kids. One year Dolph, who always loved baseball, had lost his baseball mitt. They were expensive and he didn't know how soon he'd get another one. The custom at the picnic was that all the kids ran in the races and competed in the games, and there would be prizes for everyone—usually small trinkets just for fun.

Dolph said, "I ran in my race, probably came in about fifth, and all the kids were getting their prizes—kazoos and stuff like that—and then my Uncle Bigs looks at me, points to a baseball mitt and says, 'C'mon kid, pick it up!' I don't know how he knew, but he'd found a way to get me just what I needed. I had that mitt for years."

Who knows when some kindness we do for kids—our own or others'—will radiate throughout their whole life?

> *Is there anyone among you who, if your child*
> *asks for bread, will give a stone?*
>
> **Matthew 7:9**

October 10   Things that last

We were at a wedding this past weekend. My beautiful goddaughter, who is a bright and wonderful young woman, married a bright and wonderful young man. They love each other very much. There was much joy in the church and in the reception hall as people gathered and greeted one another warmly with hugs and kisses and vigorous pats on the shoulder. We prayed together, then ate and sang and danced, knowing the joy that comes in a special way when you're happy and hopeful for a young couple in love.

Occasionally conversation drifted to troubling world events, and more than once I heard people say, "Everything's changed since the terrorist attacks." In many ways that's true. Surely our naïve illusion of universal safety has been shattered, and the threat inherent in that change brings with it anxiety, confusion, even panic to parents everywhere.

And so it was good at the wedding to spend time immersing ourselves in the things that have not changed: tender love, old friendships, loving commitment.

Who will separate us from the love of Christ?
Will hardship, or distress, or persecution, or
famine, or nakedness, or peril, or sword?

Romans 8:35

October 11   The saints as kids

I sometimes like to think of the great saints as kids. For example, one tradition has it that Saint Jude and Jesus were cousins who played together when they were young. I imagine them playing some version of kickball in one of the fields surrounding Nazareth.

I think of that scene when I see my children and their cousins running around at a holiday party, or when I get together with my own cousins—never often enough—and feel the affection and loyalty and identity I have with them. Such musing makes the saints more real to me. It makes it easier for me to believe that though the saints are already in heaven they are ready to help those of us who are still trying to make it "on earth, as it is in heaven."

It helps me to know that saints were people who had aunts and uncles and cousins and friends, just like we do. They were prone to all the trials and tribulations—as well as the joys—of living in their own time. It helps me to imagine them as young boys or girls, with all a young child's hopes and fears, wishes and dreams.

> *Ruth said, "Do not press me to leave you or to*
> *turn back from following you! Where you go, I*
> *will go; where you lodge, I will lodge; your peo-*
> *ple shall be my people, and your God my God."*

Ruth 1:16

October 12   Beyond sentiment

People of a certain type are reluctant to see in family life a primary place where faith resides. They think such a view is faulty because family life is so easy to romanticize into sentimental and sappy images seen through rose-colored glasses.

I remember my time working at an orphanage. The life these kids led was not sentimental or sappy. They'd suffered hurt, loss, abandonment and worse. And yet as the boys in my hall became family to one another, it was never hard to see the hand of God at work—in their generosity, care, protectiveness, and willingness to sacrifice for the good of others.

Yes, some people want to portray family life as all rainbows and lollipops. But that's not how most people experience it. Do we have the eyes to see what's really going on in our families? And if we do, do we then see God around our kitchen table?

> *Keep these words that I am commanding you today in your heart. Recite them to your children and talk about them when you are at home.*

Deuteronomy 6:6-7

October 13   From shame to blessing

I call it the "twinge factor"—the feeling we parents experience as old memories remind us of mistakes we have made in raising our children. The events may be long past, yet we carry inside us guilt about ways we've failed as parents.

I sense that Jesus would rather we find release from these feelings and travel free, but how do we get rid of the shame we feel? One way is to live in the land of blessing instead. This is not as difficult as you might think. Right now, this minute, no matter what you have done, Jesus invites you to live in his love. Will you allow yourself to accept that invitation?

> *I will bless those who bless you, and the one*
> *who curses you I will curse; and in you all the*
> *families of the earth shall be blessed.*

Genesis 12:3

October 14   From fear to forgiveness

I was giving a retreat and the discussion turned to forgiving people in our family. One woman who had been angry and unforgiving of her family members for many years said she'd recently come to a newfound peace. How did she do it?

"When I stopped being afraid of them, I realized I could forgive them," she said.

The room went silent as we all pondered her words.

> *There is no fear in love, but perfect love casts*
> *out fear; for fear has to do with punishment,*
> *and whoever fears has not reached perfection in*
> *love.*

1 John 4:18

October 15   Time for the present

When my daughters were younger we used to read them the Ramona Quimby books by Beverly Cleary. I remember one episode when the little heroine, Ramona, went off to a new school for the first time. The teacher was mulling over where to have her sit permanently and told her, "Sit here for the present." Little Ramona got excited thinking that she was going to get a gift if she sat where she was told. She was pretty disappointed at the end of the day when she went home empty-handed.

I think there's a lesson here for those of us who wonder if we're doing anything significant with our lives. At times a parent's lot can seem full of empty, endless, repetitive tasks—like changing diapers, making beds, cleaning up, cooking and washing dishes, all seemingly with no "present" at the end of the day.

That's when we need to look for the present—the present contained in the "now." In Ramona's case, as I recall the story, that day she spent looking for a gift-wrapped box was also the day she met some future friend and learned a number of important lessons about herself and about life.

So if today seems empty, Mom or Dad, look around for the present. It may come in a form you never would have expected.

A gift opens doors; it gives access to the great.

Proverbs 18:16

October 16   Faith, hope and charity

How do the virtues of faith, hope and charity show up in a parent's life?

We have faith that we don't raise these children alone, that we are supported by God in all we do.

We let our heart hope, despite any troubles our children might be experiencing, that all is well.

We take seriously Jesus' promise that where charity and love prevail God is always found, for we know how much we love our children.

Do you not know that you are God's temple and that God's Spirit dwells in you?

1 Corinthians 3:16

October 17   Staying close

The father and the teenage son butted heads all the time. It seemed no matter how they started out they ended up in an argument.

A friend suggested, "Maybe your son needs to be like that."

"What do you mean?" asked the father. "Why would my son want to argue all the time?"

"Well, it's his job to separate from his parents right now, and that's kind of scary for most kids. Arguing is one way of creating some distance from you while staying close to you."

"Staying close?"

"Yeah, have you ever watched Olympic wrestling? It sounds to me like you guys are always grappling, and that keeps you pretty close."

"Oh," said the dad. He had to admit his friend made some sense. But he thought to himself, "Maybe I can find another way to keep my son close that doesn't hurt so much."

> *In life and in death they were not divided; they were swifter than eagles, they were stronger than lions.*

2 Samuel 1:23

October 18   Dunked

I was watching some boys on a lake who were playing on over-inflated rafts. They were trying to climb on the rafts and stand up on top of them. Meanwhile the waves were rolling and tossing the rafts to and fro. It was an impossible task. Just when one of them would almost get upright, the raft would flip out from under them and the kid would get dunked.

When we parents try to project ourselves as totally on top of things it's like trying to climb up on our over-inflated ego and rise above the waves. Just like those kids, it doesn't take long before we end up toppling and landing with a big splash.

> *Everyone who hears these words of mine and does not act on them will be like a foolish man who built his house on sand.*

Matthew 7:26

October 19   More to the story

When I was a camp counselor years ago the kids expected me to tell a story every night. They especially loved one ongoing story I told them about a kid their age who was really a prince but didn't know it. Children want to believe there's "moreness" to their lives. And in fact it's true. Jesus said so.

Jesus was constantly telling us that we are more than we can ever dream. We have a parent in heaven who has prepared a special place for us there. He wants to give us *everything* that belongs to him. This is indeed good news.

So tell your kids stories of wonder and wild imaginings, stories that reveal the hero to be more than he or she seemed. You'll be preparing them to understand this truth about themselves—that they are indeed sons and daughters of God. This is not a mere metaphor. It's their ultimate identity.

> *For all who are led by the Spirit of God are children of God.*

Romans 8:14

When our kids become teenagers our relationship with them can alter and change from month to month. They're going through lots of emotional ups and downs, and usually we parents are too.

For example, I was feeling a bit distant from my younger daughter, Patti, as she experienced the tempest that was her sophomore year in high school, surely one of life's cruelest passages and a time when it's important to put up defenses. I felt an edge to her that belied the tender-hearted little girl I knew so well.

One day, though, we were both in the living room reading. Patti was in the midst of *To Kill A Mockingbird*. No words passed between us for quite some time. I heard a sniffle and looked up. She sat there reading with tears streaming down her lovely cheeks. My heart melted. This powerful tale of a good person standing up against injustice had touched her adolescent heart. Any fears I had about her future melted away as well. I knew my daughter was growing up just fine.

> **Let your tender mercy come to me, that I may live; for your law is my delight.**
>
> **Psalm 119:77**

October 21   Chaos and creativity

The very first passages of Genesis, the book that opens up the Bible, begin with chaos. There are formless voids with roiling waters swirling menacingly. Yet when the spirit of God hovers over chaos, life and form and purpose take shape. As I heard one artist put it, "Chaos is the medium in which God works."

Where's the chaos in your life as a parent? Know that the spirit of God is hovering there, on the brink of creation. Something good, something of God is possible from this chaos. Sit quietly, open your hands, breathe. Say, "Thy will be done."

> *In the beginning when God created the heavens and the earth, the earth was a formless void and darkness covered the face of the deep.*
>
> **Genesis 1:1**

October 22   Trying out

The son came home dejected. Though he'd practiced hard all summer, he flubbed and fumbled his way through the tryouts. He didn't want to talk about it but went to his room and closed the door.

His dad stood outside the door not knowing what to do. He did not want to make things worse, but he couldn't seem to find the words to make things better. His heart cried out, "If only you knew, son, just how much I admire you for the risks you take." He stood at the door, wondering if he should knock.

> *O Israel: Do not fear, for I have redeemed you; I have called you by name, you are mine. When you pass through the waters, I will be with you; and through the rivers, they shall not overwhelm you; when you walk through fire you shall not be burned, and the flame shall not consume you. For I am the Lord your God.*
>
> **Isaiah 43:1-3**

October 23 — Training wheels

My friend, Kathleen Chesto, calls parents the "training wheels for children." She says we parents are there to provide the balance our children need during the delicate process of growing up.

It's helpful to realize that we're not here to do all the work for our kids. We're just supposed to steady them as they learn to ride.

It's also comforting to know that once they can ride on their own they can circle back and return home.

I hereby command you: Be strong and courageous; do not be frightened or dismayed, for the Lord your God is with you wherever you go.

Joshua 1:9

October 24 — Honest?

We parents can encourage our children's ability to know and speak the truth, or we can reinforce their "hiding out" in fantasy.

For example, when a child "turns herself in," you might say, "Thank you for telling the truth. Now let's talk about what you did and learn from the experience."

Never punish a child for speaking the truth.

And the spirit is the one who testifies, for the spirit is the truth.

1 John 5:6

October 25   Get creative

Parents I talk to worry they will turn their kids off if they say too much about religion. While I believe it's possible to overdo the pressure on kids (you can never nag or coerce anyone into believing what you want them to believe), I always urge parents not to simply clam up about spiritual things.

Get creative about expressing your faith in ways that connect with your child.

> *Teach them the statutes and instructions and make known to them the way they are to go and the things they are to do.*
>
> **Exodus 18:20**

October 26   Zigging and zagging

It's a common sight: Parents take their toddlers out for a walk in the stroller, but the child wants to push the stroller. Instead of the nice, easy walk the parent had in mind, it becomes an adventure in zigging and zagging down the sidewalk with the parent trying to keep the child from running into people and obstacles along the way.

If I could just follow the ten commandments, the beatitudes, the works of mercy, then my spiritual life would be more direct, a much smoother journey. But I always want to take control and push that stroller hither and yon. This is not bad. It's the way we humans grow. Thank you, God, for being such a patient parent.

> *But you, O Lord, are a God merciful and gracious, slow to anger and abounding in steadfast love and faithfulness.*
>
> **Psalm 86:15**

October 27   Three questions

Awoman told me that before they dig in to eat dinner every night, everyone in her family who is present answers three questions: 1) What am I grateful for? 2) What am I sorry for? 3) Whom did I help today?

This little practice defines her family as one that cares.

> *Did I not weep for those whose day was hard?*
> *Was not my soul grieved for the poor?*

> **Job 30:25**

October 28   Healing

The young girl's fever got worse as night drew on. The dad, a widower, felt unequal to the challenge. It was a night of medicine, cold compresses and prayers, a night of watching and worrying. Toward morning the fever broke.

In the morning, she asked him, "Who was the lady?"

"What lady?"

"The lady standing behind you last night when you woke me up to take a drink."

"What did she look like?"

"She looked like an angel."

He sat a minute, wondering. "Maybe," the exhausted man began, "maybe that was your mom."

> *Then he said to the disciple, "Here is your mother." And from that hour the disciple took her into his own home.*

> **John 19:27**

October 29   S.O.S

Some days the best I can manage in my prayer life is this: "God help me, and God help my wife, and God help my children."

The Lord protects the simple; when I was brought low, he saved me.

Psalm 116:6

October 30   Hold the phone

Technology is a double-edged sword. It can help families stay in touch, but it can also serve to keep us apart. It's important to examine how each new piece of technology either serves family values or undermines them.

For example, my family made great strides toward sanity when we installed a telephone answering machine. We now have this simple rule: No calls during dinner. The quality of our dinner conversations greatly improved.

So the disciples set out and went to the city, and found everything as he had told them; and they prepared the Passover meal.

Mark 14:16

October 31   Who's that knocking?

Amaniac comes to my door with a hatchet in his head and blood oozing down his face. I laugh out loud and give him a high five. I drop an extra Butterfinger into his bag of booty. Next comes a fairy princess with matching glitter on her cape and eyelids. I bow before her as I drop a few Kit Kat bars into her glow-in-the-dark plastic bucket. She bestows a smile on her humble servant and lightly taps the top of my head with her silver wand.

A mixed pack of hoboes and ballerinas rambles up our steps. Football heroes and ghouls, vampires and Pocahontases, even a few "cross-dressing" cheerleaders show up. They all get what's coming to them. I greet Mr. Rogers with a bag of M&Ms, Michael Jordan with a fistful of Snickers (I'm a fan).

A hula dancer, three little pigs, Zorro, and a kid who may be a tornado victim (but pretty much looks like this all year long) arrive toward the end of the evening and hit the jackpot, each getting gobs of candy that would otherwise make my kitchen cabinet an occasion of sin.

I appreciate the joy that these children bring to my door this night. May I be as welcoming to them in our church and community in days to come.

> *The stranger has not lodged in the street; I have*
> *opened my doors to the traveler.*
>
> Job 31:32

November 1   Saints close to home

Most people know someone they would consider a saint—maybe their mother or father, their aunt or uncle, a brother or sister, or just someone in the neighborhood or parish who lives life with quiet holiness. There are all sorts of saints—rabble-rousing saints like Joan of Arc, quiet saints like Therese of the Little Flower, saints that changed the world like Thomas More and Gregory the Great, and saints who passed through life relatively unnoticed.

What distinguished all of them was how their relationship with God was primary and how they let that relationship infuse their whole life. While they remained very human, their lives were charged with divine love.

This is the challenge for all parents. Where are the saints in our life? Are we the saint in someone else's—especially our children's? Being a saint is what we are all called to be.

> **Blessed are the pure in heart, for they shall see God.**
>
>   **Matthew 5:8**

November 2   We are all souls

Today is the day we remember loved ones and others who have died. When I was a kid we were told to pray for the "poor souls" in purgatory. We were also encouraged to "offer things up" for their relief. It was a kind of bartering to get them time off for good behavior—ours!

The theology of all that can easily go awry, but the valuable and true lesson I took away from those days was that we're all connected. What I do for you can have a positive effect across space and time—even into eternity. That's a radical belief of faith. I still pray to my grandmother, asking her help in life. I pray for people who have died, especially those who were troubled at the time of their death. And I am certain of one thing: After I die, I will continue to pray for my children and perhaps in due time my grandchildren and great grandchildren. After all, how could I not?

> *In a large house there are utensils not only of*
> *gold and silver but also of wood and clay, some*
> *for special use, some for ordinary.*
>
> **2 Timothy 2:20**

November 3   Trouble

One of my favorite lines in literature comes from *Zorba the Greek* in which the irrepressible Zorba (who will always be Anthony Quinn in my imagination) is talking with his timid boss about some risky plans. The boss hesitates, worried at the prospect that they might run into trouble. Zorba responds, "Life is trouble, boss. Let's go look for trouble!"

Life often arrives accompanied by trouble of one sort or another. As parents we want to protect our kids from any kind of woe. (How often do you end your goodbyes with your kids by saying, "…and be careful!")

But while it's good we teach children caution and exercise it ourselves, there's something sacred and holy about being able to walk into life with open hands and an open heart—no matter what the risks and challenges might be. This is an act of plentiful faith responding to God's promise of abundant life.

Give your worries their due, but only their due. Then go look for trouble!

*They went to him and woke him up, shouting,
"Master, Master, we are perishing!" And he
woke up and rebuked the wind and the raging
waves; they ceased, and there was a calm.*

Luke 8:24

November 4   Come as you are

Have you seen the film *Billy Elliot*? I highly recommend it
for parents and anyone who deals with children. It's the
story of a boy, the youngest son of a widowed coal miner
in England, who comes to realize that he loves to dance. On the sly,
he starts skipping the boxing lessons his father pays for and slips
into a local ballet class, where he's the only boy. (In his gritty, working class town, no other male would be caught dead practicing ballet.)

When the father discovers his son in the dance class the old man
erupts. He simply cannot abide the fact that a son of his could do
what, in their circumstances, is unthinkable. After all, what would
the men of the town think of his son? And what would the men of
the town think of him, the father?

As parents we worry about how our kids will handle peer pressure. But we should also wonder that about ourselves. All parents
are susceptible to peer pressure. Kids instinctively know that, which
is why they wait to throw their tantrums in stores, restaurants and
other public places. *Billy Elliot* raises great questions about overcoming our susceptibility to the peer pressure that prevents us from
welcoming our children as they are, delighting in the gifts they
have, and being willing to prize even those talents and traits that
fall afoul of what society finds acceptable.

As for you, if you will walk before me, as David your father walked, with integrity of heart and uprightness, doing according to all that I have commanded you, and keeping my statutes and my ordinances, then I will establish your royal throne.

1 Kings 9:4-5

November 5   With open hands

When I was a high school teacher I had one class that used to sit glaring at me each day, sitting with their arms crossed and scowls on their faces. Needless to say, class was usually not any fun for them or for me. Luckily they were followed the next period by an exuberant bunch of students, and that class and I learned a lot together and had loads of fun. Attitude matters, and our posture can reveal our attitude.

There's a West African saying that applies to family life. "God gives nothing to those who keep their arms crossed." Every day is filled with gifts. Too often we go through life with our arms crossed, either literally or symbolically. Check out your body language today with your family. Do something that indicates you're walking through life with your arms wide open.

Then get ready for the gifts to arrive.

The Lord brought us out of Egypt with a mighty hand and an outstretched arm.

Deuteronomy 26:8

November 6 — Feelings

Parents get upset when bad or difficult things happen to their kids. Yet we can't protect our children from every one of life's harms and challenges. A wise friend told me that it's not so important what happens to kids as how well they're able to process the feelings they have about what happens to them.

As parents we need to: 1) give our children permission to own their feelings; 2) recognize that they have those feelings; 3) reassure them that we care about their feelings.

Only after those three things are accomplished can we help our children reframe their feelings in a wider perspective.

> *See, I waited for your words, I listened for your*
> *wise sayings, while you searched out what to*
> *say. I gave you my attention.*
>
> **Job 32:11-12**

November 7 — Twirling

Our first house after we were married was right across the street from the railroad tracks. I took the train that ran down those tracks to and from work. On my way home I would peer out the window of the train, hoping to get a glimpse of my kids when the train began to slow as it approached the station. Often I would see my two daughters through the big picture window in our living room, and usually they would be dancing.

Seeing them twirling around would change my whole demeanor. The cares of the day fell away. I got a bounce in my step as I hustled home. When I'd walk through the door, I would sometimes enter dancing to the strains of Mickey Mouse's *Mousercize* album or some such children's recording.

Remember the words of the great philosopher James Brown: "Any problem can be solved by dancing."

> *Then Jephthah came to his home at Mizpah; and*
> *there was his daughter coming out to meet him*
> *with timbrels and with dancing.*
>
> **Judges 11:34**

November 8   No longer draining

Being a parent is not simply one "greeting card moment" after another. It involves a lot of menial and even unpleasant chores. Once while I was scouring the bathroom getting ready for a house full of company, I had a bit of a revelation. I stopped seeing housework as a "drain" on my spirit and energy and began viewing it as an opportunity to love. Scouring the tub, dragging out the folding chairs, vacuuming and dusting the living room, bringing extra tables in from the garage all became acts of love for the people who would be entering my house in a few hours.

It was then I realized the wisdom of Saint Therese's "little way" of spirituality—the way of doing ordinary things with extraordinary love. What I learned that day was that the extraordinary love wasn't something I could manufacture. It was a gift from God that arose naturally in my heart when I gave myself fully to the task at hand. Some days I feel it more than others, but since that day I have always known that I am never far from the extraordinary love of God.

> *His master said to him, "Well done, good and*
> *trustworthy slave; you have been trustworthy in*
> *a few things. I will put you in charge of many*
> *things."*
>
> **Matthew 25:21**

November 9   What's in a name?

One task of parents is to let children know they are called to greatness. Throughout the Bible and in many cultures around the world, someone's name reveals to them a sense of their own identity and purpose.

Have you told your children why you chose the name you gave them? Whom are they named after? What significance did the name have when you selected it?

Is your child named after a saint? If so, do they know much about that saint? I know I have gained much in my life from learning the stories of Thomas Aquinas, Thomas More, and of course Doubting Thomas, the apostle who overcame uncertainty and went on to great acts of faith.

The next time you call each of your children, say their names with a sense of sacredness. After all, you are talking to a child of God.

> *He determines the number of the stars; he gives*
> *to all of them their names.*
>
> **Psalm 147:4**

November 10   What job will you do?

Years ago at work, our old computer system would come alive in the morning and this question would be the first one to greet you: "What job will you do?"

All the computer wanted to "know" was which program you wanted to access, but I always found this question an opportunity to take a moment and ponder. It's a good question for anyone to ask as you start each day.

When it comes to our children, if we can remember that the job we want to do is to launch them well into life, we're going to be less likely to get bogged down in petty concerns and give real energy to the larger questions of building their character and nurturing their faith.

What job will *you* do today?

> *Then I heard the voice of the Lord saying*
> *"Whom shall I send, and who will go for us?"*
> *And I said, "Here am I; send me!"*
>
> **Isaiah 6:8**

November 11   Faith and freedom

One of the benefits of having young kids is that you get to watch a lot of cool movies that you otherwise would miss or forget about. One of my all-time favorites remains *Pollyanna*. I'm sure I must have seen it as a kid, but it was only when I rented it to watch with my children that I came to appreciate its great vision of American life. Pollyanna surely has an idealized view of the world, but it's an ideal that's worth aspiring to in many regards.

The best scene in the movie comes when Pollyanna challenges a preacher to question his hellfire and brimstone approach to preaching and consider the "glad passages" of the Bible. The minister is worried that rich Aunt Polly, who controls the entire town because of her wealth, won't approve, but Pollyanna chides him, "Nobody owns the church." It's a simple but powerful affirmation of the freedom we should experience in religion: freedom of conscience, freedom to believe as we choose, freedom to acknowledge the truth as we see it.

Religion is often portrayed as the refuge of the fearful and the easily duped, but this bit of film shows how religion can also be a force for liberation.

*Let the heavens be glad, and let the earth rejoice,
and let them say among the nations, "The Lord
is king!"*

1 Chronicles 16:31

November 12   Secret powers

My daughters and their friends created elaborate games during the early grammar school years. One was called "Secret Powers." I could never fully comprehend the rules by which this game was played or even what the object might be. But I knew that each child could claim a secret power that would help them whenever they got in trouble.

I liked that my children played this game. They grew up with the expectation that there was surprising and unsuspected strength inside them, and I can see that strength in them today.

*Hallelujah! For the Lord our God the Almighty
reigns.*

Revelation 19:6

November 13   Daddy Bear

When my daughter, Patti, was born I bought her a white stuffed bear that had a little pocket on his chest. In the tiny pocket, attached by a string, was a little red heart. I poured all my love for her into that heart, so that it would be near her always. She called him Daddy Bear. Mostly, she loved that bear and kept him near her at all times for years.

One day, though, when she was about five and very mad at me, Patti brought Daddy Bear out to the living room and stabbed him repeatedly with a bread knife in front of me. That got my attention!

Years later I was glad she brought Daddy Bear along to college, and on the day we dropped her off at school I slipped a note into the bear's pocket telling her how much I love her. I'm not sure she ever found that note, but I know that Daddy Bear was constantly whispering to her, telling her the very same thing.

>*Be strong and courageous; do not be frightened*
>*or dismayed, for the Lord your God is with you*
>*wherever you go.*

>**Joshua 1:9**

November 14   The perfect gift

You never know when you're going to get a gift that really affects your life. I'm not sure who gave it to me, but when I was a kid someone gave me a book of children's poems. I loved that book and read it often, absorbing the rhythm of the words, carefully placed one after another in the form of songs. I learned many of the poems by heart. When I came across it years later, I felt great joy. Even today I keep the book on my nightstand and look it over from time to time.

The funny thing is, I'm not sure I ever told anyone just how much that book has meant to me. It was a secret in my heart that I have now shared with you.

I suspect there are things like that book in our own kids' lives—some gift or object that speaks directly to their soul. I believe the gifts we need find a way to us and we find a way to the gifts we need. So watch what things belonging to your children you toss. That beat up old book or doll may be more valuable to your child than a Mickey Mantle rookie baseball card.

>*Awake! Awake! Utter a song!*

>**Judges 5:12**

November 15   Moral support

When they got home from the grocery store the mother realized her daughter was getting ready to open some candy they hadn't paid for. After slowly prying the story out of her, the young girl admitted that she had taken the candy and was now sorry.

"You have to bring it back to the store and apologize," said her mom.

"Please, Mom, don't make me do that," the daughter cried.

"Honey, you can bring back the candy or bring them payment for the candy. But you have to make this right."

"Do I have to?"

"You have to do it. But you don't have to do it alone. I'll come with you."

> *Now, therefore, amend your ways and your doings, and obey the voice of the Lord your God.*
> **Jeremiah 27:20**

November 16   One hour

My dad went in for a serious medical test—a full body scan. I asked him how it went.

"The hardest part was simply lying still in an awkward position for such a long time," he said. "It helped to remember Our Lord asking his disciples, 'Could you not wait one hour with me.' I offered it up for him and for people who are suffering."

Once again my father taught me a deep religious lesson: Our lives are small and tragic only if they are not part of a larger story. When we suffer with Jesus, we will also rise with him.

He said to them, "I am deeply grieved, even
unto death; remain here and stay awake with
me."

Matthew 26:38

November 17   Finding God

I know two fine parents who raised their children in an atmosphere rich in faith, made sure their kids went to catechism
class, and prayed at home and went to church as a family. Yet
now their grown children do not attend church or proclaim membership in any faith. One of their children is a lawyer who works
among the poor. Another works for famine relief in war-torn countries. And the third is a social worker who strives to get homeless
people back on their feet.

The parents still hope their children "catch the faith." The children think that's because their parents fear they will go to hell, but
really it's because the parents hate to see them live such a good and
strenuous life without the consolations and joys that come with
faith and membership in a faith community.

They would search for God and perhaps grope
for him and find him—though indeed he is not
far from each one of us.

Acts 17:27.

November 18   The theologian

I was interviewing a famous theologian. He was a scholar and
had the look of a guy who spent most of his life in libraries surrounded by thick books. Our conversation remained academic for a while, but then I asked him about some new work he was

delving into on how people experience God's grace. His eyes lit up and his whole demeanor changed. He came alive.

As the conversation continued and I got caught up in his enthusiasm, our interview no longer seemed dull and academic. In fact, it was as if we were a couple of kids on a hot summer's day running through a water sprinkler. Every new splash of information brought us great delight.

> *Then you shall take delight in the Lord, and I*
> *will make you ride upon the heights of the earth.*
> **Isaiah 58:14**

November 19   I've been waiting for you!

One of my daughters babysits for a number of great kids, and one of her favorites is a girl named Olivia. I love to hear the exploits of this adorable and precocious two-year-old. After the recent Winter Olympics, Olivia's mom had promised to take her to an ice show where Michelle Kwan would be performing. Kwan is Olivia's absolute favorite performer. As time got closer, Olivia's mom would say, "Two more weeks and we go to see Michelle."

The day finally arrived, and Olivia and her mom wound their way through the maze of tunnels and passageways to get to their seats. When they finally got to the place where they could see the ice, Olivia stopped, looked all around, and called out, "Michelle, I'm here. I'm here Michelle."

I suspect God is as eager for our arrival as Olivia knew Michelle Kwan would be for hers.

> *Now faith is the assurance of things hoped for,*
> *the conviction of things not seen.*
> **Hebrews 11:1**

November 20   Tears

Ayoung adult I knew took his own life. My wife and I have been friends with his parents since before all our children were born. We've gone through many parental ups and downs with this couple, and as we walk into the funeral parlor my heart is straining with the heaviness I feel. I see my friends, the young man's parents. Their hearts are shattered.

The father and I embrace and his body shakes with sobs. He steps back, looks me directly in the face and says, "There's just no way I could get through this without my faith."

At that moment his faith carries both of us.

Jesus began to weep.

John 11:35

November 21   Bleak days

November in Chicago can be bleak. We can have stretches of overcast days where the sun is only a distant rumor. Nightfall comes earlier and earlier, and soon I'm leaving for work and arriving home in darkness. Then it's a quick dinner, help the kids with homework, do whatever housework needs to be done, then off to bed to repeat it all the next day.

Tonight, though the family budget doesn't allow for it, we're going out to dinner. We'll get pizza, salads, pitchers of root beer. The girls can each invite a friend. What the heck! We'll laugh, tell stories, disrupt our deadly routine.

Jesus, thank you for the example you gave of always enjoying a good meal (whether you could afford it or not).

Go. Eat your bread with enjoyment, and drink your wine with a merry heart; for God has long ago approved what you do.

Ecclesiastes 9:7

November 22   Where were you?

I was in the eighth grade when John F. Kennedy was assassinated. We had just returned from recess when our principal came on the PA system and announced our president had been shot. She led the school in saying the Rosary.

That was a traumatic day and a traumatic weekend. I know just what an impact that event had on my generation—we all can answer readily where we were when we first heard the news. And the scene of Jack Ruby stepping forward and shooting Lee Harvey Oswald at close range, replayed over and over that weekend, still seems as fresh and terrible as last night's nightmare.

Kids growing up today had a similarly disturbing and even more devastating event around which to peg the memories of their childhood. Their psyches will forever have emblazoned on them the image of huge passenger jets plowing full-speed into the side of the World Trade Center, causing the towers to collapse and fall.

We have all been treated to images of suffering and death. It's up to us parents to see that our children become sufficiently familiar with the reality of resurrection as well.

Why do you look for the living among the dead?
He is not here, but has risen.

Luke 24:5

227

November 23 — It's a date!

If there's one discipline that my family has practiced through the years it's our commitment to gathering at 5:45 each night for dinner. If we're in town and unless there's an extraordinary reason one of us can't make it home, we are all there to eat together.

This means we all have to make choices and sacrifices. For example, when I need to get more time in at work, I head in earlier in the morning rather than simply staying later.

It's a relief in many ways to have a point in the day to aim toward. There's great consolation knowing that no matter how wild my day gets or how difficult or disappointing, I will be greeted warmly and welcomed at the dinner table by my family. I am pleased I can offer them the same commitment to them.

Meals together are the heart of family life. We don't bring just our physical hunger to the table but our emotional and spiritual hungers as well. They all receive nourishment.

> *The son of man came eating and drinking.*
> **Matthew 11: 19**

November 24 — A grateful heart

The best lessons are given and taken without words. Each year at Thanksgiving, after the turkey is stuffed and placed in the oven, my family and I grab a couple of shopping bags full of canned goods and household supplies for the poor and head up to church. Despite there being no official obligation to attend this Mass, it seems the holiest day of the year to me. The church is always packed.

It's after the Scripture readings and the short homily that the silent lesson takes place. At the Offertory, the part of the Mass where we bring our gifts to the altar, an amazing event occurs. All the families in the church stand as one, grab the bags they have brought, and move forward to bring what they have to the altar: children, old people, smiling people, cranky people, rich people, poor people, some people hampered by various ailments but wanting to bring their gifts too. It's a rare glimpse of the church in action—rising up not out of duty but out of gratitude, giving what we have for the good of others, for the good of all.

Seated again, we're amazed at what our meager gifts have amounted to—bags and boxes of donations piled around the altar on every side. I see all this. My daughters sit next to me, and I know they see it too.

> *Then he said to them, "Go your own way, eat*
> *the fat and drink sweet wine and send portions*
> *of them to those for whom nothing is prepared,*
> *for this day is holy to our Lord.*
>
> Nehemiah 8:10

November 25   Feeding the hordes

When I was a kid Grandma's house was filled to bursting on Thanksgiving Day. At least a dozen of us cousins were jammed in a side bedroom to eat on an old wooden folding table. The big table in the dining room stretched out all the way into the living room, and two dozen adults found their place around its length. More kids were tucked in other bedrooms and in the pantry. The size of the crowd and the abundance of food matched the joy in our hearts at being together. After dinner the kids were shooed off to the local movie house and the adults played cards or talked in the kitchen. At the end of the day each grandchild got a huge encircling hug from Grandma and a kiss on the forehead from Grandpa. The two of them seemed magical—able to feed so many people in their modest home.

And so it wasn't that big a surprise the first time I heard that Jesus had fed 5000. I just figured his grandparents were around to help.

> *So he made them a feast, and they ate and drank.*

Genesis 26:30

November 26 — Where's Jesus?

The priest at our parish complains that too few young people are attending Mass. They don't sing; they don't come to Communion; they complain they get nothing out of the service.

And yet no youth are invited to be lectors or Eucharistic ministers. None are invited on the parish council. Their suggestions for changes in the liturgy are met with pedantic and academic responses, and when they bring their exuberance to church they receive scornful glares.

Over in the gym, on the other hand, the place is brimming with kids. With minimal guidance from adults the kids have formed teams, set up a tournament schedule, work the kitchen, sell tickets, run a raffle, and have a great time. When they think of the parish they think of the gym. Good thing Jesus hangs out there too.

> *And I raised up some of your children to be prophets and some of your youths to be nazirites.*

Amos 2:11

November 27   End times

There's a growing sense that the year is winding to an end. Days are shorter; a chill is in the air. The Sunday readings are filled with dire warnings of judgments and cataclysmic events. It seems the end of the world is at hand.

And yet in a week or so we will begin a new church year with the quiet anticipation of Advent. And so the year goes round, including and encompassing all the possibilities that humans might experience in this lifetime—and in the next.

> *Then I saw a new heaven and a new earth; for the first heaven and the first earth had passed away.*

Revelation 21:1

November 28   The first snowfall

It was a long day with too many phone calls, too many meetings, too many interruptions. My brain was about to explode. On my way home from work snow had begun to fall lightly. During dinner it began to come down in earnest. I kept a watch out the window while giving the kids their bath and getting them ready for bed. I made a few necessary phone calls and then went down to the basement to locate our old snow shovel.

I threw myself into clearing the walkways in front of our house. It felt good to have a job where I could measure my steady progress, and so I continued on to do my neighbor's sidewalk and his neighbor's as well. At a certain point I stopped and simply watched the snow tumble down.

This was the moment I was seeking: a moment of blessed stillness that brings the rest of the day into focus. In the falling of the snow I felt that grace, too, was tumbling, tumbling, tumbling, and piling up in our lives all around us.

Be still and know that I am God.

Psalm 46:10

November 29   There is a season

There are many seasons you will pass through in the course of raising your children. Wisdom is appreciating each season as it unfolds and not trying to live in the ones to come or the ones that have gone by.

God, help us to find the graces and the gifts in the season we're in today.

> *He changes times and seasons, deposes kings and sets up kings; he gives wisdom to the wise and knowledge to those who have understanding.*

Daniel 2:21

November 30   Prudence

As a parent, I'm often perplexed about what to do next. That's where prudence comes in. Prudence is the virtue that lets us know when to do something and when to do nothing.

My niece Elizabeth told us of such a time when her father, my brother Marty, knew just what to do—and that was to do nothing at all.

It was a difficult time in their family. My sister-in-law Jean was in the hospital with their newborn child, Meghan Grace. It was an extended time of disruption, and life at home was just not the same without Mom. On the way back from visiting Jean and Meghan

Grace, Marty took Elizabeth, Bridget and Brian with him to do some errands. They were running late and worry was in the background. A song came on the radio that Mom loved. As they pulled into the driveway, Marty moved to turn off the radio. But he sensed something in the moment, looked at his children in the rearview mirror, and sighed.

"He didn't turn off the music," Elizabeth told us, years later when the crisis had passed. "He let it play. He let us sit there in the van and listen to it all the way through."

The light in her eyes told the whole story: of a family that felt torn from its moorings and a special moment of grace when hope was revived and courage was shared. What Marty did was practice the virtue of prudence.

> *Blessed are the meek, for they will inherit the earth.*
>
> **Matthew 5:5**

December 1   Watch and wait

W e've entered the season of Advent, a time when we are invited to watch and wait. These two activities run contrary to the manic mood of the Christmas buying season that we are constantly urged to join.

As a parent I struggle to find balance between these aspects of Advent—one ancient and one modern. One habit that helps me stay true to the religious spirit of the season is to make a point of simply watching little kids. We once had a holiday party at our home where we invited people from church back to the house after Sunday Mass. It was a great time, with lots of congeniality and joy in one another's presence. One little boy was simply enamored with the paper plates we had bought for the special occasion. They had an old-time Santa Claus design. He was taken with this image as only kids can be. The simple, bright rendition of Saint Nicholas filled his heart with delight.

This young guy personified Advent for me. My wife leaned over and said to him, "Would you like to take one of the plates home with you?" His eyes lit up, and I got my first glimpse of the true Christmas spirit we were all waiting for.

> *Keep awake, therefore, for you do not know on*
> *what day your Lord is coming.*
>
> **Matthew 24:42**

December 2   Simplify, simplify

I n Richard Rohr's *The Wild Man's Journey: Reflections on Male Spirituality* I came across his line, "We are converted by new experiences much more than by new ideas." This squares with a current theory in education called "engaged learning." The basic idea is that students learn best by working with lessons from real life.

Advent is about more than new ideas; it really is a time to take new actions. "Make straight the way of the Lord!" cries Saint John the Baptist. "Repent!" What concrete action can you and your children take this Advent to make the pathways of your lives straighter?

For most families there's an important clue in the word *simplify*. Perhaps you can get rid of one thing you really don't need: a commitment that has outlived its usefulness, a habit that needs to be broken, a tradition that no longer has meaning, an expense you cannot afford.

> *On that day, the branch of the Lord shall be*
> *beautiful and glorious, and the fruit of the land*
> *shall be the pride and glory of the survivors of*
> *Israel.*

Isaiah 4:2

December 3   Swimming upstream

I got an e-mail from my good and wise friend, David Thomas, that inspired me to want to act differently this Advent. Maybe it will inspire you as well:

Dear Tom,

Just last night my wife Karen and I were talking about our deep ambivalence surrounding Christmas. The news has been filled with reports on whether this will be a "good" or a "bad" Christmas season—which, translated, means the amount consumers spend on gift giving. What's tragic is the totality of this reporting. Nothing else gets on the screen. Like millions of others—a silent majority of sorts—Karen and I are trying to simplify Christmas so that the feast is more filled with family and friends just coming together to celebrate life. We've cut back on decorations and parties. The number of gifts has been reduced. (Still to be determined is the role of fruitcake this year!) It's a time for great decisions, and none are easily made. Swimming upstream is always hard. I wish you and your family your best Christmas ever.

David

> *Blessed shall you be in the city and blessed shall you be in the field.*
>
> **Deuteronomy 28:3**

December 4   All I want for Christmas

A common question our family members ask one another this time of year is, "What do you want for Christmas?"

It pays for us parents to think about this question on a deeper level, however. What is it that you really want in your life: peace, courage, serenity, consistency, holiness, patience, humility? Why not ask God for that particular gift, and then become aware of all the ways that gift is already being given to you?

If you know what your heart wants and ask for it in joyful hope, you will be more open to the possibility that the gift is already yours for the taking.

> *For everyone who asks receives, and everyone who searches finds, and for everyone who knocks, the door will be opened.*
>
> **Matthew 7:8**

December 5   Advent glow

O ur late next door neighbor, Harold, was a good man with deep spiritual passion, but he practiced no religion. One December day he called me aside and asked, conspiratorially, "What's been going on in your house lately?"

"What do you mean?" I asked, wondering what he was talking about.

"I'm not peeking, mind you, but I couldn't help but notice through your kitchen window at dinner time that it's all dark and then you've got some candles burning. What's up?"

I told him it was our Advent wreath and explained that we start each dinner with a song and lighting of one candle for the first week, then two the next week, up to four the final week before Christmas.

Harold looked at me seriously and said, "That's a good thing, Tommy. Keep doing that."

> *You are the light of the world. A city built on a hill cannot be hid. No one, after lighting a lamp puts it under the bushel basket, but on the lapstand, and it gives light to all in the house.*
>
> **Matthew 5:14-15**

December 6   Silent Night

Sometimes I think little kids have a survival instinct that warns them when they're pushing their parents over the edge. Today, after a long day of sibling rivalry, whining, sassing and bad attitudes all around, the climate in our house changes dramatically as darkness falls.

It's as if a heavy storm front had been hovering all day and has now moved on, leaving clean, fresh breezes in its wake. As bedtime comes the family sits together reading books and playing with toys. I breathe a sigh of gratitude.

> *Let us come into his presence with thanksgiving.*
>
> **Psalm 95:2**

December 7   Stories to live by

I hope you and your family will be getting your fill of good holiday stories this season. Though typically aimed at children, these stories are often variations on themes from the original Christmas story. For example, you will find stories of self-giving, like "The Gift of the Magi" or "It's a Wonderful Life"; or stories of unlikely heroes, like "A Charlie Brown Christmas" or "Rudolf the Red-Nosed Reindeer"; or change-of-heart stories, like "A Christmas Carol" or "The Grinch Who Stole Christmas."

In the next few days to come, as the magic of the season intensifies, take time to enjoy a Christmas story together with your kids. It can be a story you read together or a video or program you watch on TV. Or better yet, it might be a story from your own youth that you share with your kids. Tell them about the best gift you ever received and why it meant so much to you, or about your most memorable Christmas and what made it so.

> *An angel of the Lord appeared to Joseph in a dream and said, "Get up, take the child and his mother, and flee to Egypt, and remain there until I tell you: for Herod is about to search for the child, to destroy him."*
>
> **Matthew 2:13**

December 8   Hail, Mary

Mary, the mother of Jesus, looms huge in Christian imagination and religious practice. She is "the one who said yes," the one who bore God in her womb, the one who prepared him and presented him to the world, who insisted that he perform his first miraculous intervention at Cana.

Mary was the first witness: to his birth, to his life and teachings,

to his death. "Mary kept all these things in her heart," the gospel
says. It surely was an amazing heart. That's why so many parents
turn to her as a model, consoler, intercessor and source of strength.

> *And he came to her and said, "Greetings,*
> *favored one! The Lord is with you."*
>
> **Luke 1:28**

December 9   Emmanuel, "God-with-us"

Where do we see "God-with-us" today? Perhaps you see
God:

- in the antics of a two-year-old who sets the whole
  family laughing;
- in the sorrow of a family whose child has died and whose memory they hold precious;
- in the memories conjured up with each ornament you put on
  your tree;
- in the dedication of an old man who cares so tenderly for his
  wife whose Alzheimers grows worse by the year;
- in the selfless courage of the police officers and firefighters who
  gave their lives trying to save others in the collapsing towers of
  the World Trade Center;
- in the energy and creativity that comes with doing one's life
  work well;
- in the merriment of a gathering of neighbors, family or friends
  celebrating the holiday, or in a car full of teenagers on their way
  to sing carols at an old folks' home;
- in the preacher who digs deep to find words of life and power to
  touch the hearts of people who come to church just one day a
  year.

Therefore, the Lord himself will give you a sign.
Look, the young woman is with child and shall
bear a son, and shall name him Immanuel.

Isaiah 7:14

December 10   Christmas cards

E ach day's batch of mail brings more Christmas greetings, some from very far away. As part of our prayer at dinner my family reads the cards and messages from people we love and who love us. Some messages bring good news; some bring sadness. We share the stories with our kids of how we came to know these people, how we're related, what they mean to us. In the light of the Advent wreath our warm family circle grows.

Comfort, O comfort my people, says your God.

Isaiah 40:1

December 11   Preparation

T his morning at Mass I sat across the aisle from a very pregnant young lady. The Advent readings on "prepare the way" took on deeper meaning as I watched her leaning back in the uncomfortable pew.

This woman will spend a lot of her parenting career preparing: setting up a nursery, signing kids up for preschool, running out late at night for forgotten science project supplies. But the best preparation for parenting she can make is the one she is doing this morning: attending to her own inner spiritual state.

A voice cries out: "In the wilderness prepare the way of the Lord, make straight in the desert a highway for our God."

Isaiah 40:3

December 12   Guadalupe

Today is the feast of Our Lady of Guadalupe. Her image shows up everywhere in my urban neighborhood. There she stands—pregnant, expectant, full of God, aware of herself, aware of me. No matter what happens, she does not look away. I think how reassuring her presence must be to recent Mexican immigrants whose lives have been disrupted, who come to a city whose ways are strange and sometimes harsh. She is the mother who is always there.

> *My soul magnifies the Lord, and my spirit rejoices in God, my Savior.*

Luke 1:47

December 13   Christmas gift, part 1

In the spirit of the carol, "The Twelve Days of Christmas," here are twelve gifts you can give your kids right up to Christmas Eve.

Whenever I ask parents what their biggest stress around the holidays is, they always mention lack of time. There never seems to be enough to do everything they want to do, and during the Christmas season this is especially so. So of all the gifts you can give your children this year, the most precious may be your time. Find a way to give at least ten minutes of uninterrupted time each day to your children. Let it be their time to talk, be quiet, ask questions, play a game.

> *Stand at the crossroads, and look, and ask for*
> *the ancient paths, where the good way lies: and*
> *walk in it, and find rest for your souls.*
>
> **Jeremiah 6:16**

December 14   Christmas gift, part 2

Have you gotten so busy and preoccupied that you seldom laugh? Share some laughs with your kids. You know what tickles their funny bone and yours. Make merry with your children several times before Christmas.

> *Make a joyful noise before the King, the Lord.*
>
> **Psalm 98:6**

December 15   Christmas gift, part 3

Telling stories is what makes us human. People tell stories to make sense out of life, to share values, to give clues to who they really are at the deepest level. Telling stories is a great way to pass on your faith and your values to your children. Take time to read or tell some of your favorite stories to your children during this Christmas season. Better yet, create your own Christmas stories together.

> *Now the birth of Jesus, the Messiah took place*
> *in this way. When his mother Mary had been*
> *engaged to Joseph, but before they lived together,*
> *she was found to be with child from the Holy*
> *Spirit.*
>
> **Matthew 1:18**

December 16   Christmas gift, part 4

Patience is in short supply during the holidays. Emotions are running high. Excitement is building. You as the parent can set the tone by showing extra patience to your kids. This is not easy. You may want to ask God for help. Remember the classic prayer: "God, grant me patience—and I want it *now*!

> *Happy are those who persevere.*
>
> **Daniel 12:12**

December 17   Christmas gift, part 5

I heard a story about how kids at a playground can tell which parents go with which child. "Just look for which kid each parent is yelling at," they say.

Every day before Christmas make at least one physical show of affection to each of your children—a hug, a smile, a pat on the back, a chance to sit on your lap. This is one gift that has a great return policy too. Whatever you give out you're likely to receive more in return.

> *Set me as a seal upon your heart, as a seal upon*
> *your arm; for love is strong as death.*
>
> **Song of Solomon 8:6**

December 18   Christmas gift, part 6

What most homes need as Christmas approaches are moments of serenity. Faith is the foundation of serenity. Faith lets us know that we will be okay no matter what is going on. Say the serenity prayer throughout the day and share the fruits of that prayer with your children: "God, grant me the serenity to accept the things I cannot change, the courage to change the things I can, and the wisdom to know the difference."

> ***Better is a handful with quiet than two handfuls***
> ***with toil, and a chasing after wind.***
>
> **Ecclesiastes 4:6**

December 19   Christmas gift, part 7

One Christmas season I was walking through downtown, head bowed, mind on many things. A little kid got off the bus with his mother, stopped in his tracks, looked around, and cried, "Wow! Who did all *that*!" For the first time that season I noticed the bright lights and decorations up and down Chicago's famed State Street.

See if you can experience some "wow" with your kids this week. Visit the Christmas lights in your town, attend Midnight Mass, take a walk at night and look at the millions of stars.

> ***Great are the works of the Lord, studied by all***
> ***who delight in them.***
>
> **Psalm 111:2**

December 20   Christmas gift, part 8

One of the most poignant moments of the first Christmas story was when Joseph approached the inn and was told, "There's no room for you."

In many ways we parents communicate to our own children, "There's no room for you." Make space for your children this Christmas by giving them opportunities when they can have your full attention. Look them in the eye. Follow up what they say with questions that show you're interested in what they feel.

Here's a tip: If you have paid attention to your own feelings and needs, you'll find this gift much easier to give.

According to the promise that I made you when you came out of Egypt, my spirit abides among you: do not fear.

Haggai 2:5

December 21   Christmas gift, part 9

T he central message of the Advent story is that in our darkness we have "seen a great light." Light is a big part of Christmas celebration. Spend a good stretch of time with your kids sitting in the dark, with just the lights of the Christmas tree or the candles on the Advent wreath. You can play Christmas tunes in the background, or simply be quiet. You don't have to say too much about the symbolism, either, for light itself speaks powerfully to children.

On this, the shortest day of the year, when the days have shrunk and the darkness threatens to envelope us, celebrate light.

The light shines in the darkness and the darkness did not overcome it.

John 1:5

December 22   Christmas gift, part 10

W e threw a party for all the people from my workplace and their families. Everyone brought a special dish to share and there was plenty of food and drink. The fire

was crackling in the fireplace. The buzz of conversation grew bois-
terous and clusters of people would erupt in laughter. Kids mingled
with the adults and slowly got to know the other kids. Soon they
were laughing and playing games together. At one point a violin,
guitar and accordion appeared and we sang Christmas Carols. I realized then just how great it is for our children when our work
friends become our family too.

> *And suddenly there was, with the angel, a multi-*
> *tude of the heavenly host, praising God and say-*
> *ing, "Glory to God in the highest heaven, and*
> *on earth peace among those whom he favors!"*
>
> Luke 2:13-14

December 23   Christmas gift, part 11

When thinking about gifts it is sometimes better to think
about experiences rather than things. Experiences stay
with you forever. A while back my wife and I began a
tradition of giving the four of us a Christmas gift to enjoy as a family. We decided that each holiday season we would go to a play.
Live theater is a great gift. It lifts the spirit and feeds the soul. Having this history of shared theatrical experience strengthens our family bonds and brings us great joy. We've seen joyous plays and sad
plays, deep plays and frivolous plays. We always have a good time
and lots to talk about afterward.

> *My heart exults in the Lord; My strength is ex-*
> *alted in my God.*
>
> 1 Samuel 2:1

December 24   Christmas gift, part 12

Being with extended family is sometimes a challenge and especially so at Christmas. At a time that urges closeness and joy, some families feel distance and pain. As a last gift to your children this Christmas season, try to get them together with their grandparents, aunts, uncles and cousins, even if it takes extra effort, expense and energy. (If you can't physically be together, spend time on the phone or with photo albums or videos.)

There's bound to be pain in every relationship. Even the story of Jesus' birth is tinged with discord, rejection, and even violent death to the innocents at the hands of Herod. Can joy flower amidst such pain? That is the essence of the Christmas story. Even as we celebrate his birth, we know what hardships faced Jesus in his life, but on this holy night we let our joy have its day, knowing that this new birth will, in due time, make all things calm, all things bright.

> *When they saw that the star had stopped, they*
> *were overwhelmed with joy.*
>
> **Matthew 2:10**

December 25   In the manger

Mary and Joseph had their baby in a stable and laid him in the manger, a food trough. Many people gathered around. What did they see?
- The three wise men saw light in the darkness.
- The poor saw food for the world.
- Shepherds saw a good shepherd who would lead his sheep.
- Farmers saw a vine that connects humans to the source of life.
- A townswoman saw a fountain of living water.

- Angels saw the glory of God.

Bring your children to visit a manger. Help them develop the eyes to see all there is to see there.

> *This will be a sign for you: you will find a child*
> *wrapped in bands of cloth and lying in a*
> *manger.*
>
> **Luke 2:12**

December 26   Green Jell-O

Now, you need to know that I'm a picky eater and was even worse when I was a kid. At big family gatherings, it was not surprising to see me come back from a table groaning under the weight of dozens of tasty options with just a slice of bread, two pickles and some potato chips on my plate. My Aunt Nora knew I liked green Jell-O with pineapple in it. On special McGrath family occasions she would always make Jell-O and make sure I loaded up on it. Even into my adulthood, when Nora would bring Jell-O to family gatherings she'd give me a wink. It was our inside joke, and just one example of the love my aunt had toward all us kids.

The Christmas after Aunt Nora died we were all missing her. When her daughter, Mary Therese, walked in with the green Jell-O with pineapple in it, I felt an excruciating mixture of great loss, gratitude and comfort all at once. It was the best Christmas gift I got that year. Like Jell-O, there's always room for signs of love.

> *Then, opening their treasure chests, they offered*
> *him gifts of gold, frankincense, and myrrh.*
>
> **Matthew 2:11**

December 27   Snow bundle

When she was about six my daughter, Patti, was scheduled to stay over at her friend Mimi's house. They had been looking forward to it all week. That day, however, snow began to fall early and built up all day. By the time I got home from work traffic was snarled and streets were closed.

Patti was feeling terribly disappointed, but we wrapped her up in her snow suit and scarf and plopped her on her sled, and off we headed to Mimi's house, a mile or more away. It was quiet without any traffic, and I would turn back and check on Patti and I think she may have been smiling under all those wraps. Her eyes were bright and shiny and twinkled like the snow swooping down beneath the street lamps.

I delivered her to Mimi's house, and Mimi was ecstatic to have a playmate in this wondrous snowstorm. I was grateful to have had this wonderful adventure with my child.

> *You know that in the Lord your labor is not in vain.*
>
> **1 Corinthians 15:58**

December 28   Over but not out

Christmas day has come and passed but it needn't be absent from our lives the rest of the year. One step you can take to welcome Jesus into your life is to begin each day with prayer or quiet time. It needn't take long. The key is to simply put aside all other worries for a short time and start your day opening your heart to the presence of Jesus.

Family life offers plenty of ways to serve God and deepen your spirituality. But those opportunities can easily slip by if you don't start out the day with the right frame of mind.

Make a habit to find a time of prayer first thing in the morning or some other regular time. It will make a huge difference in the quality of your days.

> *The Word became flesh and lived among us, and we have seen his glory, the glory as of a father's only son, full of grace and truth.*
>
> **John 1:14**

December 29   The bright, shining sun

It's bleak in Chicago. For days now it's been overcast and cold and snowy. It's hard for me to believe that elsewhere in the world the sun is shining and the sky is blue.

I am consoled by a lesson I learned the very first time I flew in an airplane. We took off on a dreary day, one of dozens in a row we'd had that winter. And I remember the surprise (and delight) I felt when we broke through the clouds and the bright, shining sun greeted us and the blue sky stretched for as far as the eye could see.

God, help me teach my children that no matter what's going on in their lives right now there's more to the story. Somewhere the sun is shining. Let that somewhere be in their hearts.

> *The sun rises and the sun goes down, it hurries to the place where it rises.*
>
> **Ecclesiastes 1:5**

December 30   Holy families

Last week at Christmas families gathered all across the country. Some dined on fine china, some on everyday dishes, some on paper plates. Some huddled in lines at soup kitchens, and some visited through thick glass at a jail or prison.

With love and yearning, great expectations and forgiveness, sorrow and joy, they all made their attempts at being a holy family.

God bless us, every one.

> *Be strong and bold: have no fear or dread of*
> *them, because it is the Lord your God who goes*
> *with you: he will not fail you or forsake you.*
>
> **Deuteronomy 31:6**

December 31   Even now

Throughout my years as a parent I have occasionally worried that I would not be up to the task—that my meager efforts would fall short of what my kids required of me. My friend Sister Sheryl Chen, who is a Trappistine nun, gave me an image to hold on to that fills me with hope.

One December morning when she awoke for early prayers she wandered outside the monastery and was struck by the brilliance of the stars. Looking at one particularly bright star, she calculated its distance and how long it took for its light to reach her on this early morning. She was struck with how the light of the star, streaming down to shine on her face, was like the love of God. Even before we need it, God's love is on its way to meet us in our hour of need or want.

So do not fear about tomorrow. Whatever challenges you will face, God's love is—even now—winging its way to meet you, to strengthen you, to bless you, to surround you and your children in God's all-embracing grace.

> *They set out, and there, ahead of them, went the*
> *star that they had seen at its rising, until it*
> *stopped over the place where the child was.*
>
> **Matthew 2:9**

Other Books of Interest to Parents

Daily Meditations (with Scripture) for Busy Moms
Patricia Robertson
The perfect book for every mom you know. 368 pages, $9.95

Daily Meditations (with Scripture) for Busy Dads
Patrick T. Reardon
For dads of every age with kids of any age. 368 pages, $9.95

Daily Meditations (with Scripture) for Busy Grandmas
Theresa Cotter
Let's not leave grandma with nothing to read! (368 pages, $8.95)

Our Common Life
Reflections on Being a Spouse
Mary and Rob Glover
Over 100 reflections for married couples. 120 pages, $5.95

Christmas Presence
Twelve Gifts That Were More Than They Seemed
Gregory F. Augustine Pierce, ed.
Author Tom McGrath contributed "Dad's Gift," one of twelve wonderful stories about the deeper meaning of holiday gift giving in this Christmas classic. 160 pages, hardcover, $17.95

**Available from booksellers or call 800-397-2282
in the U.S. or Canada**